WHY

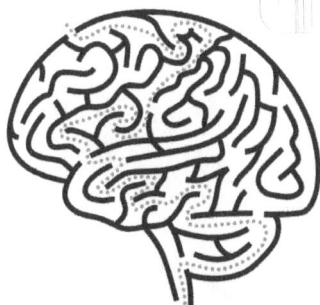

YOUR KIDS
DO WHAT
THEY DO

Published by Four Rivers Media

For foreign and subsidiary rights, contact the author.

Cover design by Sara Young

Cover photo by Gabriela Furtado

ISBN: 978-1-959095-15-6   1 2 3 4 5 6 7 8 9 10

Printed in the United States of America

RODNEY GAGE

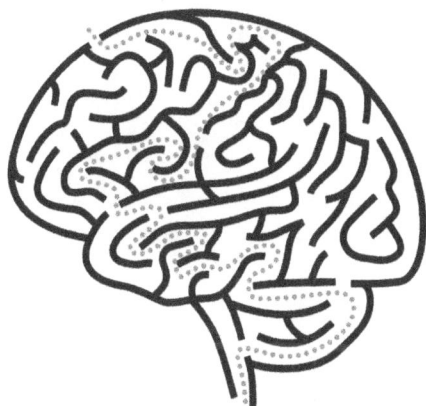

WHY
YOUR KIDS
DO WHAT
THEY DO

**RESPONDING TO THE DRIVING FORCES
BEHIND YOUR TEEN'S BEHAVIOR**

**FO
UR**

This book is dedicated to every parent who is in the trenches of raising the next generation. You are doing better than you think you are, and you matter more than you think you do. Your greatest contribution in life may not be something you do but someone you raise. Remember: Life is short; live intentionally. Life is long; stay encouraged.

CONTENTS

PART III. KNOWING AND LOVING EACH OTHER

FOREWORD

One of the great tragedies of our society is the negative and often destructive behavior displayed among today's youth. Problems like teen pregnancy, teen suicide, alcohol and drug abuse, gender confusion, and gang violence dominate the headline news. Most concerned parents and adults find themselves asking those "why" questions regarding the motives behind such negative and destructive behavior. Even problems like defiance, withdrawal, and anger are often displayed among today's churched youth which can leave Christian parents baffled as to why their kids do what they do.

In my years of working with young people, I'm convinced that there is a legitimate reason behind every wrongful act and attitude displayed among youth. One of those reasons is unmet emotional needs in their lives. Studies show that our key emotional needs have a profound effect on the way we think, feel, and ultimately behave. Fortunately, that is what this book is all about. One of America's dynamic Christian leaders, who really knows and understands teenagers and has successfully raised three of his own, has taken the time to share his insights with parents who are in the process of raising the next generation.

In *Why Your Kids Do What They Do*, Rodney Gage gives answers to all those "why" questions you're probably asking or will ask one day about your kids. As a parent, you will find this book packed with practical solutions and application-oriented advice to help you understand how to identify and meet your teenager's most important emotional needs. In fact, you will not only better understand your teenager, but you also will learn a lot about yourself in the process.

I pray that parents and church groups will take advantage of utilizing this powerful resource. I truly believe the body of Christ and families will be much better prepared for life because of this timely book.

—Josh McDowell

ACKNOWLEDGMENTS

Anytime you take on a project of this magnitude, you have to recruit the right people to make it happen. The first person I called was my dear friend Martijn van Tilborgh with Four Rivers Media. We have worked on numerous publishing projects together. His team is simply the best! Thank you, Sarah Petelle, for your patience and willingness to go the extra mile to serve and support the needs of this project from start to finish.

To my wonderful ReThink Life Church family. I am so honored to be your pastor and cheerleader as we all continue to run our race with endurance—the race God has set before us in this life of faith.

Last, but certainly not least, thank you to my amazing wife, Michelle, of over thirty-two years. You have gracefully modeled intentionality and unconditional love to me and to our three amazing children and two sons-in-law. You practice daily what it looks like to love like Jesus. Your encouragement, inspiration, and support are what keep me going to pursue my passion for helping families win.

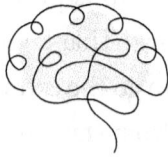

HOW TO USE THIS BOOK

D o you remember going shopping for your kids when they were little? I remember buying our oldest daughter, Rebecca, her first big toy. We bought her a brand new Little Tikes Grand Coupe Car. I remember carrying that big box inside our house and setting it in the middle of our living room floor to assemble. On the outside of the box was a color picture of the car, and in big bold letters it said, "Easy assembly, no tools required."

For the next three and one-half hours, I used every tool in my garage except a chainsaw to put that car together. My little girl must have said a million times, "Daddy, is it ready yet?" You had to be a rocket scientist to figure out how to assemble that car. I finally gave up and put the half-assembled car back in the box and drove back to the toy store where I bought the thing. I offered a teenager who worked at the store twenty bucks if he would help me put it together. It took the teenager all of five minutes to assemble the car and collect his tip. (Who says teenagers don't amount to anything)? I must confess the process probably wouldn't have been so hard if I had listened to my wife and read the directions thoroughly.

This book has lots of easy instructions that are guaranteed to help you build lasting relationships with your kids. However, you must be willing to take the time to work through the individual chapters and exercises. I pray you will make it a priority to let God use you to be the number one influence in your teenager's life. As you journey through this book, there will be many opportunities for you to interact with your teenager. I encourage you to take it slow. Don't try all the techniques outlined here on the first day. It's going to take time for you to establish these principles in your relationship. However, if executed properly, it will happen sooner than you think.

Apart from individual time you invest, I highly recommend working through this material with your spouse or another parent of a teen. The most effective way to gain insight, strength, and encouragement is through small groups. Experts agree that one of the strongest methods to enrich relationships happens in small groups. Let me encourage you to gather together some other parents and offer to host a small group in your home or someone else's home and work through this content and masterclass together. You can use the personal study guide for group discussions.

I trust this book, its study guide, and the masterclass will be used to form life-giving relationships in your home and church.

PART 1

UNDERSTANDING YOUR TEENAGER

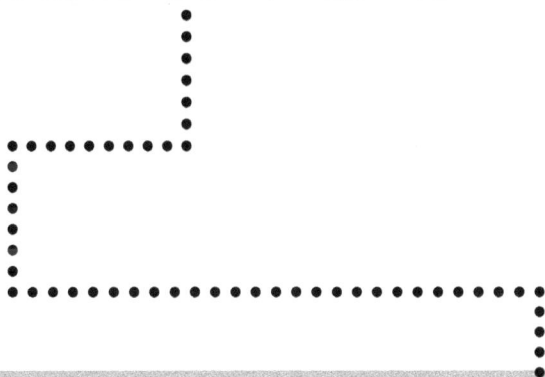

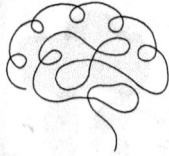

WHY YOUR KIDS DO WHAT THEY DO

I will never forget an incident that took place during my junior year of high school. One of my good buddies and I were driving home one night from downtown Dallas. We had gone to a Dallas Mavericks basketball game. After fighting through the massive traffic jam after the game, we finally got onto the freeway that took us toward our side of town. I was driving a brand new Datsun (Nissan) 280ZX (Google it) that belonged to my dad. Since it was a school night, we were instructed by our parents to get home immediately after the game.

Being the two obedient, responsible young men that we were (slight exaggeration), we both agreed it would be best if we obeyed our parents by quickly returning home—emphasis on quickly. I thought it would work to our advantage to get us home faster if we pushed my dad's sports car to the limit. Therefore, as we got on the freeway, I eased up behind a pickup truck that was traveling about 85 mph. If you've ever been in a sports car that sits low to the ground, 85 mph feels like you're just barely moving. So I decided to move over into the next lane and put the pedal to the metal.

At this point, I was traveling about 100 mph. We noticed the guy in the pickup truck put the pedal to the metal as well. Before we knew it, he was right beside us, obviously wanting to race. I looked over at my friend Dave and said, "I feel the need for some speed." We were now reaching speeds of 115 to 120 mph. As I reflect back on that night, I honestly believe that as a seventeen-year-old kid, the thought of having a wreck or putting my life or my friend's life in danger never entered my mind. All I wanted to do was to leave that pickup truck in the dust. As my friend Dave and I were celebrating by giving each other a high five, as though we had just won the Daytona 500, out of nowhere, I saw flashing red lights in my rearview mirror. Not one but two police cars were in sight.

Getting a speeding ticket was one consequence I failed to think about as I was traveling a smooth 120 mph down the freeway. Not only did the police pull us over they pulled the guy in the pickup truck over as well. Being that I am a preacher's kid, I had heard my dad quote Numbers 32:23 (KJV) a million times: "Be sure your sin will find you out." Boy, did it ever! Fortunately, the police officer showed mercy and compassion toward me by issuing my first-ever speeding ticket for only 105 mph. I must confess, however; my parents were not so compassionate and merciful after I mustered the courage to tell them three days later.

As a parent, have you ever wondered why teenagers do the things they do? Surprisingly, what appears to be risky or bizarre behavior to adults makes perfect sense to teenagers. Teenagers see nothing wrong with their abnormal behavior. Yet, would a sane, rational adult:

» Drive 120 mph down the freeway to show off in front of his friend?
» Break up with her boyfriend via text after being in a "relationship" less than a month to "avoid the pain of breaking up later when it will hurt more"?
» Drink from the milk jug and then assure his mother, "It's okay. I'm not sick"?
» Look at a room piled high with clean and dirty clothing, books, papers, and empty bags of chips, then ask, "Where's my phone?" (Well, maybe a few adults would do this!)

You get the picture. Every day, adolescents act strangely while adults shake their heads, wondering what's wrong with teenagers today.

• •

EVERY DAY, ADOLESCENTS ACT STRANGELY WHILE ADULTS SHAKE THEIR HEADS, WONDERING WHAT'S WRONG WITH TEENAGERS TODAY.

• •

But what about the behaviors that really frighten parents?

In a recent survey conducted by Pew Research following the COVID-19 pandemic, 40 percent of US parents with children younger than eighteen say they are extremely or very worried that their children might struggle with anxiety or depression at some point. In fact, mental health concerns top the list of parental worries, followed by 35 percent who are similarly concerned about their children being bullied. These issues trump parents' concerns about other physical threats to their children, the dangers of drugs and alcohol, teen pregnancy, and getting in trouble with the police.[1]

The CDC reports a 60-percent increase over the past decade in high school girls seriously considering or planning suicide or experiencing high levels of sadness.[2] The mental health outlook for teenagers across the board over the past decade has become even bleaker. Overall, 42 percent of high school students report persistent feelings of sadness or hopelessness, and 22 percent seriously considered attempting suicide.[3] The number was even higher among the LGBTQ+ students, with 45 percent seriously considering or attempting suicide.[4]

Dr. Marc Siegel, a medical contributor for Fox News, states, "Social media has a lot to with the mental health issues facing today's youth."[5] And according to *The Wall Street Journal*, "40

1 Rachel Minkin and Juliana Menasce Horowitz, "Parenting in America Today." *Pew Research Center's Social & Demographic Trends Project*, 24 Jan. 2023, https://www.pewresearch.org/social-trends/2023/01/24/parenting-in-america-today/.

2 "U.S. Teen Girls Experiencing Increased Sadness and Violence," *Centers for Disease Control and Prevention*, 13 Feb. 2023, https://www.cdc.gov/media/releases/2023/p0213-yrbs.html.

3 "Adolescent Mental Health Continues to Worsen," *Centers for Disease Control and Prevention*, 13 Feb. 2023, https://www.cdc.gov/healthyyouth/mental-health/index.htm.

4 "Adolescent Mental Health Continues to Worsen . . ."

5 Maria Lencki, "We're in Trouble with Teen Girls: Dr. Marc Siegel Analyzes CDC's 'Shocking' Teen Mental Health Report," *Fox News*, 13 Feb. 2023, https://www.foxnews.com/media/dr-marc-siegel-cdcs-shocking-teen-mental-health-report-trouble-teen-girls.

percent of teens said their sole purpose for posting on social media is to look good to other people, while 32 percent of teenage girls felt that Instagram only worsened their body insecurities."[6] From obesity to anorexia, from video games to social media, from identity and gender confusion to social isolation, from mental health disorders to alcohol and drug abuse, and from sexual promiscuity to violence, teenagers are hurting and confused now—more than ever—spiritually, mentally, morally, emotionally, and socially.

Whether it's normal (although strange) teenage behavior or the unhealthy, destructive, inappropriate actions and choices teens make, I believe the answer to all those *why* questions can be summed up in one word—needs. Like all of us, teenagers have real, significant, identifiable emotional and relational needs. I am convinced these basic emotional needs are the driving forces that motivate teenagers to do the things they do.

I have invested over thirty years in helping youth and their families. I have had the privilege of speaking to over two million students in public and private schools across America, and I have spoken to tens of thousands of teenagers at major youth events, conferences, and camps. As a local church pastor for over twenty years, I have worked with hundreds of families and counseled countless numbers of youth from virtually every walk of life. I have talked with teenagers who use drugs, who are sexually active, who get drunk regularly, who identify as LGBTQIA—"lesbian, gay, bisexual, transgender, queer/questioning (one's sexual or gender identity), intersex, and asexual/aromantic/agender"[7]—who

---

6 Emmett Jones, "Increased Use of Social Media Takes Mental Health Toll on Teens," *Fox News*, 17 Sept. 2021, https://www.foxnews.com/health/social-media-mental-health-body-image-toll-teens.

7 "LGBTQIA Definition & Meaning," *Merriam-Webster*, https://www.merriam-webster.com/dictionary/LGBTQIA.

are members of gangs, who are behind bars in juvenile detention, and even teens who have attempted suicide.

From the most defiant to the most withdrawn, I've asked these young people the "Why?" question. Many have long defensive answers for their choices and negative behavior. However, when I peel back the layers of the facade in the lives of these teens, and they get transparent with me, almost always, the root problem behind their negative attitudes, choices, and behaviors is unmet needs in their lives. More specifically, unmet needs at home.

• •

WHEN I PEEL BACK THE LAYERS OF THE FACADE IN THE TEENS' LIVES, AND THEY GET TRANSPARENT WITH ME, ALMOST ALWAYS, THE ROOT PROBLEM BEHIND THEIR NEGATIVE ATTITUDES, CHOICES, AND BEHAVIORS IS UNMET NEEDS IN THEIR LIVES. MORE SPECIFICALLY, UNMET NEEDS AT HOME.

• •

Recently, some of my dearest friends went through a crisis with their seventeen-year-old daughter that changed their lives forever. My friend Bob has two beautiful daughters from his first marriage. When Bob divorced his wife, his two girls were teenagers. Shortly after his divorce, he remarried. Now he has two small children from his second marriage. Feeling the pain of a broken home and the pain of no longer feeling important, Tracy, Bob's younger daughter from his first marriage, began to cope with her pain the best way she knew how.

Growing up in a wealthy home, Tracy had everything a teenager could ever want. She drove a brand-new sports car and wore the latest styles of clothing. Tracy always felt the pressure to keep up with her older sister who was "Miss Everything." Because of the demands of raising two new daughters and the demands of his successful career, Bob had very little time to give to his two older daughters. In his mind, he thought that since they were teenagers, they were old enough to take care of themselves as long as he took care of them financially. Bob's ex-wife continued to live nearby; however, like Bob, she had distanced herself from her two daughters due to addictions she was struggling with in her own life.

As the oldest daughter graduated from high school and moved off to college, Tracy found herself oddly living with her dad, her stepmother, and two baby half-sisters. Tracy immediately latched on to friends for attention and support. At times, she would stay out all night, never bothering to check in with her father. In Tracy's mind, she reasoned, *If my mom and dad don't care, why should I care?*

On many occasions, Tracy would tell her father she was going to spend the night with a particular friend her father knew and trusted, but instead, she would end up staying out all night with another set of friends. As you can imagine, Tracy's life was headed in a downward spiral. Tracy began drinking and using drugs. To her, this was meeting the need she had for attention and acceptance.

One day, my wife and I noticed that Tracy had lost an unusual amount of weight. It was obvious that something was wrong. I confronted Bob one day while playing golf and said, "Bob, tell me what's going on with Tracy." I told him that my wife and I had noticed she had not been herself the past few times we had been around her. I could tell Bob was concerned as well. It appeared to me that he knew what was going on but really didn't want to know the extent of it.

He finally confessed that Tracy was using drugs. He said, "Lately, when I try to talk with Tracy, we usually end up in a verbal knock-down-drag-out. I have done everything I know to do. I have threatened to take her car away. We have grounded her. Nothing seems to be working." Several weeks later, I received a phone call from Bob. With panic in his voice, he said, "Rodney, I need a favor. Can you recommend a good treatment center for Tracy? The doctors have informed us that Tracy has a cocaine addiction."

After she returned home from the treatment center, Bob called me and asked if I would meet with him and Tracy. For the first time, Tracy was able to share with her father the feelings that had caused her to rebel into a lifestyle of drug abuse that nearly took her life. She confessed that all she really wanted was to feel loved and significant. With all the attention given to her older sister and two baby half-sisters, as well as the trauma of her parents' divorce, she felt like her life didn't really matter anymore.

Using drugs was the only way she knew how to cope with her pain and get her daddy's attention. Bob and Tracy agreed to get some solid Christian counseling. Even though it's been an uphill climb, God has brought healing and restoration to their lives and family. Unfortunately, my friend had to learn the hard way that teenagers who can't find attention, support, acceptance, approval, and affection at home will seek out other alternatives to get those needs met in their lives.

Teenagers will do whatever it takes to escape from the feelings of rejection, hurt, or pain brought to their lives, whether the hurt has been caused by their parents or their friends. Therefore, in the mind of a hurting teenager, it seems perfectly normal to latch on to a group of friends whose behavior and values are negative, even destructive, as long as those people offer acceptance, approval, and attention.

IN THE MIND OF A HURTING TEENAGER, IT SEEMS PERFECTLY NORMAL TO LATCH ON TO A GROUP OF FRIENDS WHOSE BEHAVIOR AND VALUES ARE NEGATIVE, EVEN DESTRUCTIVE, AS LONG AS THOSE PEOPLE OFFER ACCEPTANCE, APPROVAL, AND ATTENTION.

Throughout this book, you will see that when a teenager's basic emotional needs are met in the home, chances are far greater that the teenager will behave in a positive, productive, healthy way. You will also discover that when a teenager's key emotional needs are ignored or unmet, that teenager will often turn to negative influences and behaviors in order to get his or her needs met. Unfortunately, for many parents who are busy and pulled in a million different directions, it's hard to know whether their teenager's needs are being met or not.

A teenager doesn't wake up one day and say, "I think I will start using drugs today," or "I think I will become anorexic today," or "Today is the perfect day for me to get pregnant by my boyfriend." Teenagers who end up making bad decisions or doing destructive things admit that there were certain feelings and insecurities they had about themselves, their family, or their friends that drove them to make bad choices in life.

As long as their kids are making fairly good grades and not causing trouble, many parents take that as a sign that everything is okay. On the other hand, if a teenager is creating trouble for the family, and there is a consistent pattern of negative behavior, parents usually take what seems to be the most natural and logical step to correcting the problem: grounding the teenager for life. I'm not saying there is anything wrong with enforcing consequences for inappropriate behavior. However, when things seemingly are headed in a downward spiral with your teen, and he or she is not responding to your efforts to correct their behavior, rather than trying to change their behavior, you may want to take a step back and ask yourself as a parent, *What are the needs behind my child's deeds? What are they trying to tell me through their negative attitudes and behavior?*

• •

PARENTS CAN MAKE A POSITIVE DIFFERENCE IN THE LIVES OF THEIR TEENAGERS BY CREATING A HOME ENVIRONMENT THAT WILL ENSURE THEIR TEENAGERS' NEEDS ARE EFFECTIVELY AND CONSISTENTLY BEING MET.

• •

Parents can make a positive difference in the lives of their teenagers by creating a home environment that will ensure their teenagers' needs are effectively and consistently being met. In chapter 2, I identify five basic emotional needs that must be met in order for teens to develop into healthy, mature adults. As you will see, I have taken the word "needs" and devised an acrostic to give you a visual tool to keep in mind as you attempt to meet your teenager's needs. The list is not exhaustive; it's just focused on specifics that address the issues teenagers face most frequently. The five basic emotional needs we will be referring to throughout this book will function as "emotional gauges," much like the gauges on your car. These gauges will serve as indicators to help you determine whether or not your teenager's needs are being met.

In chapter 3, you will discover six false assumptions parents usually make about their teenagers' needs. Also in this chapter, you will learn six ways to monitor the emotional gauges of your teenager. In chapter 4, I reveal eight different masks teenagers wear to hide their unmet needs. Chapter 4 also will help you discover the six different roles parents play that sabotage their relationships with their teens. In the final section of chapter 4, I will give you a family stress test to help you determine the key factors that might be contributing to the unmet needs in your teenager's life. Chapter 5 is pivotal because of four key relationship skills that will help you connect with your kids.

In the second part of this book, "Understanding Yourself," I will help you sort out your own emotional needs. When *your* key emotional needs are met, you will be far more successful at meeting the needs of your teenager. Unfortunately, your unmet needs can make it difficult to meet your teenager's needs effectively. As parents, we must realize that we can't give what we don't have. As we journey through this section of the book together, I will offer you some encouraging help in understanding your own needs and how to get those needs met in Christ-centered ways.

In the final part of the book, "Knowing and Loving Each Other," you will find specific actions to take to meet your teenager's needs. In chapter 10, you will discover six parenting styles that often block communication with teenagers. I will also share nine different ways to listen to your teens.

Do you find yourself having continuous conflict with your teenager? Don't worry; you're not alone. There are five steps that you can take to reduce and resolve conflict with your teenager. I will also share some tips on what to do if your teenager won't talk. Most of all, by reading the final section of this book, you will learn how to establish a relationship restart with your teenager, just like my friend Bob experienced.

To develop a healthy relationship with your teenager, you may have to deal with some issues in your own life that are influencing the way you relate to your teenager. Chapter 11 gives you some specific ways to identify your hurts and also shows you four important keys to experiencing true forgiveness and healing in all your relationships. Chapter 12 discusses why it's so important to have relationship goals with your teens.

• •

TO DEVELOP A HEALTHY RELATIONSHIP WITH YOUR TEENAGER, YOU MAY HAVE TO DEAL WITH SOME ISSUES IN YOUR OWN LIFE THAT ARE INFLUENCING THE WAY YOU RELATE TO YOUR TEENAGER.

• •

It is my prayer that when you finish reading this book, you will know how to look beyond the surface behavior of your teenager and discover specific needs that dictate your teen's overall attitudes and actions. You will see how a proactive approach to parenting your teenager will prepare him or her to become a mature, healthy adult. I promise you that the results of trying this life-giving approach to raising your teenager will be extremely rewarding. My wife, Michelle, and I have successfully raised three children to adulthood who are faithfully serving God in their own unique callings. The greatest joy we have at this season in our lives is watching them thrive in their own faith, friendships, and circles of influence.

The Bible says children are a reward from God. (See Psalms 127:3.) Do you feel like you've been rewarded? If you are having a tough time with your teenager, you may feel like children, or at least teenagers, are a curse. I want to help you change that feeling and perspective. By the time you finish reading this book, you will begin experiencing these benefits and many more as you meet the needs of your teenager in your day-to-day living. I'm convinced that you will see your teenager as a blessed, significant, and unique reward from God.

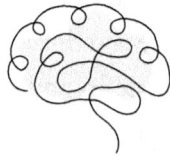

CHAPTER 2

THE FIVE EMOTIONAL GAUGES OF A TEENAGER

D o you remember the story in the previous chapter about the speeding ticket I received while driving my dad's new sports car? Well, before the speeding ticket, my dad used to let me drive his new sports car to school. When I drove into the parking lot at school, I thought I was the BMOC (big man on campus). That car was beautiful. On the outside, it was painted silver and blue. Being that I am a big Dallas Cowboys fan, it was the ultimate car. It had a gray cloth interior and an awesome stereo. It had every kind of bell and whistle you could get on a car. It even had a T-top. (Google it if you don't know what that is).

The most amazing thing I remember about that car was that it literally could talk (this was before Alexa or Siri). When the car was low on gas, a female voice from within would say, "Fuel level is low." If you didn't shut the door completely, the voice would say, "Door is open." The little lady who lived inside that car could tell you anything you wanted to know about that car. The only thing she couldn't do was drive the car for you.

Wouldn't it be great if our kids came equipped with gauges, much like the gauges on the dashboard of a car, that would indicate when something was wrong? Imagine a light that blinks on and off through your teen's eyes, indicating "Affection level is low," "Security level is low," or "Encouragement level is low."

Unfortunately, when the emotional needs of teenagers get out of whack, their gauges usually flash warnings through inappropriate, often destructive, behavior. Sometimes, their gauges will indicate that there is something wrong through silence or withdrawal and isolation. Occasionally, a teenager can verbalize a need like, "Why can't you like me the way I am?" Unfortunately, most can't.

• •

AS ADULTS, AND PARTICULARLY AS PARENTS, WE MUST BE SENSITIVE TO A TEENAGER'S BASIC EMOTIONAL NEEDS AND DETERMINE WAYS TO MEET THOSE NEEDS.

• •

As adults, and particularly as parents, we must be sensitive to a teenager's basic emotional needs and determine ways to meet those needs. Studies show that when a teenager's needs are met through healthy relationships with parents and other caring adults, teenagers will be more likely to have positive attitudes and behavior. When that happens, the emotional gauges that monitor need to return to quietly monitoring the system known as a teenager. Before we look at the five emotional gauges that will help us identify the specific needs of your teenager, I think it's important for you to understand why teenagers are so needy.

AND YOU THOUGHT YOU HAD NEEDS!

When we think of needs, we have a tendency to focus on the needs of infants and small children. Others might focus on the needs of the elderly. The truth is, no matter what age we are, we all have physical, emotional, and spiritual needs. However, when you mix in the everyday growing-up developmental needs of teenagers, suddenly, they are overwhelmed with neediness. Take a look at these key developmental areas.

. . . .

THE TRUTH IS, NO MATTER WHAT AGE WE ARE, WE ALL HAVE PHYSICAL, EMOTIONAL, AND SPIRITUAL NEEDS.

. . . .

Physical Growth

As kids' bodies begin to change and grow, it creates awkward, uncoordinated, embarrassed, and confused teenagers. It probably seems like yesterday those new jeans fit your son; today, those same jeans reach above his socks. Tennis shoes no longer wear out; they "grow out." Physical development can be spasmodic, quick, uneven, and often painful. Hearts and lungs double in capacity, and stomachs increase almost one-third in size. (You already knew this because you've watched the grocery bills climb!)

Skin eruptions like pimples can be a teenager's worst nightmare. And whatever part of the body makes the teenager the most uncomfortable is the part that he or she tries to cover up or tugs at or constantly complains about. Parents must be careful not to confuse attitude with growth. Rapidly growing teenagers are like small babies who also grow quickly—both need a lot of sleep! Don't confuse your teenager's need for sleep or the companion feeling of being wiped out with laziness, especially if your teenager has grown several inches over the last three to six months.

Sexual Growth

Sexual growth stirs deep feelings from guilt to amazement. Teenagers are one big walking hormone. Guys think about sex; gals think about love. Hair crops up in strange places. Swelling buds become breasts, and hips fill out in girls. Guys face new experiences like wet dreams and a surprisingly squeaky voice. (Have you ever noticed how thirteen- to fifteen-year-old guys rarely answer the phone?) Sexual changes prepare a teenager for sexual experiences, but he or she lacks the maturity to accept the responsibility associated with sexual intercourse. Hormones not only relate to sexual development but also influence ricocheting emotions and bizarre behavior.

Emotional Growth

As a teenager grows emotionally, the teen (and the parents) embark on a huge emotional roller coaster ride of exaggerated feelings. A simple "Good morning!" can bring a flood of tears or a tongue-lashing about *nothing* being good in this world. The greatest joy can be followed quickly by anger. Parents operate from a disadvantage unless they assume that everything is a crisis in the life of the teenager because, to the teenager, it usually is.

Social Growth

In social development, the teenager moves from a same-sex, best-friend relationship of younger youth to a circle of friends where the teenager interacts with both sexes. One intriguing area to watch in social development is how teenagers try on different personalities to see which feels comfortable and how others respond. "Today I'm going to get along with everyone," Callie announced one morning. That personality change lasted until her younger brother spilled his milk into her book bag. Notice that teenagers play to an imaginary audience. They worry about what others say about them, how others see them, and what others think about them. This self-centeredness of younger youth gradually gives way to an awareness of others as the teenager gets older.

Mental Growth

Mental growth doesn't necessarily involve the amount of information a teenager is learning but the way that information is processed. Younger teenagers are concrete thinkers, seeing life in basic terms: right or wrong, black or white, true or false. Gray areas confuse them. Around the eighth grade, teenagers begin to process thoughts abstractly. Other people's beliefs and opinions expand their thoughts and challenge their way of thinking. In the transition from concrete thoughts, where everything is one way or the other, to abstract thoughts, where nothing is known for sure, teenagers face doubt and indecision.

• •

MENTAL GROWTH DOESN'T NECESSARILY INVOLVE THE AMOUNT OF INFORMATION A TEENAGER IS LEARNING BUT THE WAY THAT INFORMATION IS PROCESSED.

• •

Mental changes sometimes make it difficult to focus on one topic at a time, and it can create poor communication skills. Many parents panic during a teenager's early mental development when their child who brought home good grades suddenly becomes academically challenged. Some of this academic change involves a teenager's struggles with mental development. A teenager's rapidly growing body, new sexual stirrings, shifting relationships, desire for independence, and fear of the unknown—all these areas cause stress that stretches a teenager to the point where school becomes a minor priority. Rather than attacking your teenager for poor grades, determine the number of changes occurring in your teenager's life to see how these might be influencing school progress.

Spiritual Growth

Another roller coaster of highs and lows can occur in spiritual growth. A younger youth who has been exposed to biblical absolutes through home and church might begin to question those beliefs and values as he's exposed to secular humanism and moral relativism at school. Social relationships affect how teens feel about themselves and how they perceive God feels about them. Teenagers who experience their faith through their parents must struggle to find a faith of their own. Doubts can be very real. Some youth feel they let God down with their doubts; others use their doubts as an excuse to bail out on religion. Through all their seeking runs their quest for values and standards that fit the person they want to become.

Stay aware of what normal physical, emotional, mental, social, and spiritual changes your teenager faces. Once they begin to look like adults, parents tend to forget that these young people still struggle with other developmental issues. Knowing what's going on will help you in judging what emotional needs they require.

AUTHENTIC NEEDS

If you ask teenagers what they need, most would say a car, money, the latest video game, a smartphone, a faster computer, and other physical items. These are wants—not needs. Needs cannot be met by things. A car cannot meet a teenager's need for affection. Money cannot meet a teenager's need for empathy. The truth is God has created us with needs so that we might constantly look to Him, allowing Him to meet our needs directly or indirectly through others.

The Bible tells us in 2 Corinthians 1:3-4 that He is "the God of all comfort, who comforts us in all our troubles, so that we can comfort those in any trouble with the comfort we ourselves have received from God." Since God created us with needs, He desires for us to look to Him—the ultimate supplier of our needs—in order to get our needs met. The Bible tells us in Philippians 4:19,

"My God will meet all your needs according to his glorious riches in Christ Jesus." As God graciously meets our needs, He wants us to unselfishly meet the needs of others.

•••

AS GOD GRACIOUSLY MEETS OUR NEEDS, HE WANTS US TO UNSELFISHLY MEET THE NEEDS OF OTHERS.

•••

In their book *Top 10 Intimacy Needs*, Dr. David Ferguson and Dr. Don McMinn use a perfect illustration of meeting each other's needs:

Because we all have needs, we need each other! It's like having an itch in the middle of your back. You can't scratch it, but someone else (who has the same out-of-reach itch) can. Therefore, you seek a fellow back-scratcher. When the two of you scratch each other's back (meet each other's needs), you both feel loved and cared for, and the relationship experiences a new and wonderful dimension—Intimacy.[8]

As you seek to meet your teenager's needs, it's important that you know what these needs look like. I've taken five basic needs that are critical to a teenager's emotional development and made them into an easy-to-remember acrostic. The list is not comprehensive, but I believe these basic emotional needs are the driving forces behind our teens' behavior. Every teenager has a need:

---

8 David Ferguson and Don McMinn, *Top 10 Intimacy Needs* (Austin, TX; Intimacy Press, 1994).

1) to be   Noticed
2) to receive   Encouragement
3) to receive   Empathy
4) to receive   Direction
5) to receive   Security

Let's look at each of these as a gauge that will help you know what is needed in your teenager's life. These gauges are expressed from the teenager's point of view. Take time to evaluate how the needs listed below relate to you and your teenager. Since there are no right or wrong answers, try to be honest in your responses. The final page of this chapter is an evaluation to share with your teenager. Use this evaluation to determine your teenager's top needs. If your teenager doesn't want to take the evaluation, don't force the issue. You are trying to build a relationship along with understanding.

1) The Noticed Gauge

"I need to receive focused attention because I am respected as a person, valued for who I am, and appreciated for what I do."

This gauge has several parts that measure the importance of being noticed:

Attention—Too often, we barely focus on the person standing in front of us, much less on a teenager who hides in her room or one whose busy schedule keeps him out of the house. How do teenagers get attention? Hair or clothing choices may be one way. Picking on a younger sibling may be another. How about their loud music? It says, "I'm here! Just wanted you to notice that!" Thump! Boom! Boom! Angry words, slamming doors, and even the dreaded silent treatment all scream for attention. Unfortunately, the attention these actions draw can be more negative than positive. Teenagers may settle for negative strokes rather than no strokes at all. This, however, is not the attention needed.

Focused attention begins with the basics of communication: turn off the TV, make eye contact, listen—don't talk, and repeat feelings you hear expressed. Focused attention validates the life of your teenager by saying, "You are worth my time, effort, and energy. You are worth it!" Wow! Can you imagine your favorite sports figure, artist, YouTuber, or movie star calling you and saying, "I want your opinion on this, please. I'd like to hear your views. And, by the way, tell me what's going on in your life." Wouldn't you feel really special? If they could get your undivided, focused attention, so should your teenagers.

» Describe the last time you gave your teenager your undivided attention.
» How did you feel about the experience?
» How do you think your teenager felt about the experience?
» In what other ways do you pay attention to your teenager?
» On a scale of 1 (low) to 10 (high), how would your teenager gauge the need for attention?

Respect—Disrespecting others, what some teens refer to as "dissing," is a popular behavior among young people. They learn this disrespectful attitude by copying morally absent personalities on television and in video games or mimicking their disrespectful peers at school. Even though our kids may laugh at the caustic comments and crude actions on reality TV or video games, as parents, we can't lower ourselves to that behavior in our homes. If we want our teenagers to be respectful, we must model respect and honor in the home. Just as much as parents want their kids to respect them, teenagers want respect from their parents. This can take a number of different forms.

Do you knock before entering a room with a closed door? Do you respect what is in your teenager's room—a cell phone or tablet, diary or journal, notes or magazines? Unless you can link a dramatic change in behavior with a pattern of defiance and disobedience or some other warning action, you should respect your teenager's things, just like you want them to respect yours.

How about your teenager's ideas and opinions? Do you respect their feelings, perspectives, or differing points of view? Do you ask your teenager for input into activities that involve them? Do you listen to what they say, even when the opinion they express today changes tomorrow? (Remember: they are trying on different personalities to discover who they are.)

Do you respect your teenager's personhood? Do you avoid put-downs, name-calling, and all teasing that belittles teenagers? Ephesians 4:29 says, "Do not let any unwholesome talk come out of your mouths, but only what is helpful for building others up according to their needs, that it may benefit those who listen." Are you careful about when you discipline your teenager? For example, do you talk to your teenager in private rather than in front of her friends?

➤ Describe a time when respect was a problem between you and your teenager.
➤ How did you feel about the experience?

» How do you think your teenager felt about the experience?

» Were you able to resolve the issue? How?

» In what ways do you show respect to your teenager?

» On a scale of 1 (low) to 10 (high), how would your teenager gauge the need for respect?

Valued—Teenagers want to be valued as people. Since teenagers are in the process of becoming, matters of character, values, standards, and personal qualities are forming. Yet, even while the teenager tests and accepts or rejects these issues, the teenager wants to feel that he or she is someone special. That specialness doesn't come from external beauty but from internal qualities—someone whose character can be admired. You value your teenager because we are valued by God, and your teenager was created by God.

Karen's mom overheard her say, "I'm not going to talk about it." There was a pause, and then, "If you keep talking about it, I'm hanging up. Goodbye." She noticed Karen wasn't angry, just forceful.

As Karen returned her phone to her back pocket, her mom asked, "I thought you were talking to Jessica."

"I was but not right now. I don't want to talk about what she wanted to talk about."

"What happened?"

"Jessica's spreading this rumor about another girl at school. I don't like rumors. I'm not going to listen. Stuff like that ends up hurting someone. I just told Jessica I'd talk to her later when she can talk about something else," Karen replied.

"Good for you!" her mom exclaimed with a hug for her daughter.

➤ Describe the last time you showed your teenager you valued him or her.

➤ How did you feel about the experience?

➤ How do you think your teenager felt about the experience?

➤ In what other ways do you value your teenager?

➤ On a scale of 1 (low) to 10 (high), how would your teenager gauge the need to be valued?

Appreciated—Value shows attention to a teenager because of the teenager's character and standards. Appreciation shows attention to a teenager because of the teenager's performance. The enemy of appreciation is being taken for granted. Teenagers feel ignored and overlooked when no one recognizes when they do a job well. They want to be appreciated for their accomplishments. Educators know that praise is a great motivator. When a person is recognized for an accomplishment and praised for that work, they are more likely to repeat the positive behavior. Unfortunately, parents expect certain behavior and forget to thank the teenager or acknowledge the work when a task is completed, especially if done well.

Appreciation starts with recognizing that a task has been completed. This might be regular chores or a special activity. Appreciation can be expressed for the completion of a task or the teenager's positive attitude toward the task. Expressing appreciation can be verbal, both privately to the teenager and publicly to others. Try to "catch" your teenager doing something right; then applaud that teenager verbally and often. I believe the five most important words a parent could ever say to their teen are "You did a great job."

» Describe the last time you told your teenager you appreciated him or her for doing a job well.

» How did you feel about the experience?

» How do you think your teenager felt about the experience?

» In what other ways do you show appreciation to your teenager?

» On a scale of 1 (low) to 10 (high), how would your teenager gauge the need to be appreciated?

2) The Encouragement Gauge

"I need to be encouraged as I reach for my dreams and supported when I feel like giving up."

This gauge has two parts that measure the importance of encouragement:

Nurture—Nurturing is the active part of encouragement. It cultivates—develops—the dreams, hopes, and goals of your teenager. Although these dreams may be unspoken, every teenager thinks about the future. For younger teenagers, these dreams may only be about what will happen this weekend. Older young people look at life beyond high school. Nurturing includes helping the teenager define and set a goal and providing a structure that allows the teen to meet that goal.

Dreaming is the easy part; making the dream happen takes encouragement that is both emotional and physical, whether it's financial support, exposure to different resources, vocational counseling, job opportunities, or a variety of experiences. Most parents want to help their teenager's dreams become a reality. Unfortunately, other parents want their own dreams they failed to reach to be achieved by their teenagers.

••

MOST PARENTS WANT TO HELP THEIR TEENAGER'S DREAMS BECOME A REALITY. UNFORTUNATELY, OTHER PARENTS WANT THEIR OWN DREAMS THEY FAILED TO REACH TO BE ACHIEVED BY THEIR TEENAGERS.

••

During her childhood years, Autumn stunned people with her impressive talent at the piano. She won contest after contest until her sophomore year in high school. One day she stopped practicing. She fought with her parents about entering competitions. She even refused to play the piano for guests and other gatherings. Finally, her parents let Autumn stop her piano lessons. They grieved over their daughter's "lost" talent. Quickly, however, Autumn discovered another talent she had as an artist. Today, Autumn is a commercial artist who incidentally loves to play the piano.

Occasionally, a teenager will struggle to define his or her dream. I believe parents can help their teens to see themselves not as they are but as they can be. Build off of the gifts and abilities you see in your teenager. Point out ways people use their gifts and talents to make a difference in the world. Expose him to people with different hobbies or professions who might spark a dream in his imagination.

Todd wanted to be an architect. He talked about applying to a top-notch engineering college that had a four-year architecture program. What concerned Todd's family was his lack of interest or ability to do math. Todd's dad worried aloud, "I'd be afraid all of

Todd's buildings would fall down!" Finally, Todd's parents asked if he would go to a vocational counselor for testing and suggestions. Todd was actually relieved when he found that architecture was not his strongest skill; arguing was. Todd is currently getting his law degree and jokes about defending architects.

- ➤ Describe the last time you nurtured your teenager's dream.
- ➤ How did you feel about the experience?
- ➤ How do you think your teenager felt about the experience?
- ➤ In what other ways do you nurture or encourage your teenager?
- ➤ On a scale of 1 (low) to 10 (high), how would your teenager gauge the need to be nurtured or encouraged?

Support—Although they are similar, nurturing begins in the present to prepare for the future, and support occurs mostly in the present. Support can involve a physical commitment. I played a lot of tennis when I was growing up, even in high school and college. Even though my dad traveled out of town a lot, I often would look up in the stands and see him join my mother late in a match. His determination to catch an early flight back home, so he could make it to my tennis match gave me the support I needed and often gave me the determination to fight back to win a match that I may have otherwise lost due to feeling tired and defeated. His support gave me the boost I needed to not only finish the match but win the match.

Support can also involve verbal or written encouragement. Two modern inventions that enhance the way we can show support to our teens are sticky notes and the smartphone. Use sticky notes of encouragement in your teenager's school books, on the bathroom mirror, on a favorite piece of sports equipment, or in a shoe. You can also send text messages of inspiration, prayers, and Bible verses to affirm your love, encouragement, and support.

Times when teenagers need support might be the night before a big test, the day they take SATs or another standardized test that determines their future, when they try out for the team, or when they are going to participate in a special event. Offer support when times get rough, when they don't think they'll finish the project, when they're experiencing a bumpy relationship, or when they get discouraged for whatever reason. Be there for your kids when it really matters the most.

» Describe the last time you showed your support for your teenager.
» How did you feel about the experience?
» How do you think your teenager felt about the experience?
» In what other ways do you support your teenager?
» On a scale of 1 (low) to 10 (high), how would your teenager gauge the need to feel supported?

3) The Empathy Gauge

"I need to receive comfort when I experience pain, sorrow, or despair."

Comfort—Comfort is one of the greatest needs teenagers have, yet few can articulate this need. Rarely does a teenager walk into the house and announce, "I've had a bad day. Will someone please comfort me?" However, your teenager may slam through the house or sulk to the bedroom. The slumped shoulders and downcast eyes of their body language tip off their discouragement or despair. Teenagers hurt emotionally much of the time. Parents yell at them. A friend moves away. Friends break trust. The "in" group rejects them. Parents and teachers demand academic excellence. A broken relationship can even create the same traumatic grief for a teenager as a physical death. Parents may also underestimate the sorrow that comes from the death of a pet, especially with younger youth.

When Jenny's dog died of old age, Jenny stayed in her room for several days. She couldn't bear to walk through the rooms or places in the yard where her beloved pet had slept, eaten, and played for twelve of Jenny's fourteen years of life. Jenny's parents helped her with her grief by urging her to talk about the funny things she liked about her dog. Comfort came when Jenny and her mom put together a photo album of pictures and funny remembrances.

Comfort is sometimes hard for a parent to give. Some teenagers are embarrassed by their emotions and prefer to hide the hurt. Others expect parents to give advice instead of just offering comfort. A few teenagers struggling with their rapidly developing bodies don't feel comfortable being hugged or touched—even by a parent. You have to figure out how to comfort your teenager almost by trial and error.

» Describe the last time you comforted your teenager.

» How did you feel about the experience?

» How do you think your teenager felt about the experience?

» In what other ways do you comfort your teenager?

» On a scale of 1 (low) to 10 (high), how would your teenager gauge the need to be comforted?

4) The Direction Gauge

"I need to feel a sense of significance and purpose in my life."

Significance and Purpose—The number one question teenagers ask during their developmental years is this: "Who am I?" Who am I physically, sexually, and emotionally? Who am I in my relationships, in my faith, and in my values? Though teenagers may not articulate those basic questions about their lives, they do want assurance that their presence on earth is important and valuable to someone. They don't want to feel like a big zero, like someone's *mistake*. They fear being labeled the *failure* in the family.

In the same way that teenagers try on different personalities to see which one fits the best, they also try on different projects to see which helps them feel significant. Some adults see this shifting from project to project as a lack of commitment, but usually, teenagers are just trying to figure out what works for them. If teenagers don't see themselves as significant in a positive way, they may look for ways to be significant in a negative, more risky fashion.

Teenagers believe they can make a positive difference in the world if given a chance. They are determined to learn from their parents' mistakes and to make the future better. These teenagers can serve in the community, through the church, or at their schools. Activities like mission trips and service projects teach the teenager the value of life and the importance of making a difference. Families who work together with their teenagers on service projects model for their teenagers how to achieve significance and purpose.

• •

**I TRULY BELIEVE THE PASSION I HAVE
IN MY HEART FOR REACHING HURTING
YOUNG PEOPLE HAS GROWN OUT OF THE
EXPERIENCE OF SEEING MY DAD INVEST HIS
LIFE INTO THE LIVES OF OTHER PEOPLE.**

• •

While I was growing up as a preacher's kid, I remember traveling with my dad to participate in many of his evangelistic events. My dad always went the extra mile to reach out to the down-and-outers. In fact, for many years, my father ran a boys' home in downtown Houston, Texas, called "Pulpit in the Shadows." It was a home for runaways and drug addicts. On many occasions, my dad would take me to the boys' home where I would meet many of the people who had given their lives to Christ as a result of my father's ministry. I truly believe the passion I have in my heart for reaching hurting young people has grown out of the experience of seeing my dad invest his life into the lives of other people. His encouragement challenged me to make a spiritual impact on my generation.

- ▸ Describe the last time you helped your teenager feel a sense of significance and purpose.
- ▸ How did you feel about the experience?
- ▸ How do you think your teenager felt about the experience?
- ▸ In what other ways do you help your teenager feel a sense of significance and purpose?

➤ On a scale of 1 (low) to 10 (high), how would your teenager gauge the need to feel a sense of significance and purpose?

5) The Security Gauge

"I need to feel physical security as well as acceptance, regardless of my flaws and mistakes, and loved no matter what."

This gauge has several parts that measure the importance of security:

Security—In addition to offering a safe environment, most teenagers want some kind of boundaries that give them specific limits in their actions while allowing them some freedom and independence. They also need help defining and setting personal boundaries in their lives as they get older.

One of the greatest challenges we all face in today's world with technology is being overexposed to virtually everything imaginable. Technology is perhaps the greatest source of distraction and temptation we face not only as adults but even more as teenagers. As you know, a teenager's world revolves around social media, FaceTime, texting, video games, the internet, and even doing homework—all on a single device that fits in the palm of their hand. Technology is all-consuming and even addictive. Therefore, we need to help our kids set limits and boundaries around technology for their own mental health and well-being. Here are five ways:

1) Set clear expectations. If parents are paying for the phone, be very specific when setting expectations. You may elicit complaints, but clearly communicating what you expect now is better than confusion later. Parents should have

access to passwords, usernames, and any other security features of the phone in the event of an emergency. Establish house rules for "tech-free zones" where phones/tablets are not allowed, such as meal times, family time, bedtime, etc.

2) Set parental controls right away. Get familiar with their device yourself, and set up parental controls and tracking features on their phones. Get alerts sent to your phone to monitor their activity. Remember: your teenagers want to have the same freedoms all their friends have. However, while they are under your roof and under your authority, they must be held accountable for being trustworthy by showing responsibility. Communicate to them that the reason why you're providing a phone for them is not for their convenience and benefit but for yours as a parent.

3) Set time limits on use. Your teens could spend hours on their devices, but that doesn't mean they should. Decide how much time your teenagers should be spending on their devices and for what purposes. Communicate those limits and expectations clearly to them. If necessary, enforce screen time limits with an app's help.

4) Check in regularly about what your kids are seeing and doing online. Even with all of our intentionality, sometimes, things slip through, and our kids end up seeing and interacting with something or someone they shouldn't. If necessary, ask to see their phones if there is anything that could cause concern or suspicion or that goes against your values, standards, and expectations as a family.

5) Enforce technology breaks. Devices are scientifically designed to be habit-forming. Research shows that the

same parts of the brain fire up when someone is on a device as when they're experiencing pleasure of some kind.[9] Make sure to factor in consistent, weekly breaks from technology (this is something that could be helpful for you too). And while you're taking a much-needed pause, plan an alternative to how that free time will be spent.

Security also means offering your teenager a hedge against others who might threaten or harm him or her. Bullying, human trafficking, and violence are all major issues of concern for both teens and parents. They cause fear, anxiety, and insecurity that can paralyze our kids on many levels. This is why keeping open communication, tracking our kids' locations, and being aware of whom our teenagers are associating with are so important. Our teenagers need to know we are not snooping behind their backs or trying to control them. It's a matter of providing them with extra security through our love and support by showing them we love them enough to care.

• •

OUR TEENAGERS NEED TO KNOW WE ARE NOT SNOOPING BEHIND THEIR BACKS OR TRYING TO CONTROL THEM. IT'S A MATTER OF PROVIDING THEM WITH EXTRA SECURITY THROUGH OUR LOVE AND SUPPORT BY SHOWING THEM WE LOVE THEM ENOUGH TO CARE.

• •

9 "Neuroscience of Screen Time: Dopamine Pleasure Pathways," *Carrots&Cake*, 9 Nov. 2022, https://carrotsandcake.com/dopamine-pleasure-pathways/.

Another side of security is providing a stable environment. An unstable environment may be caused by dysfunctional parents, job changes, shifting economics, a move to another place, the addition of grandparents to the household, or the serious illness of a family member. When Sarah's parents divorced shortly after she turned thirteen, Casey, Sarah's closest friend, feared that her own parents would divorce, too, although her parents' marriage was strong. Casey needed regular assurance that her family would remain intact.

➤ Describe the last time your teenager felt secure because of something you did or said.
➤ How did you feel about the experience?
➤ How do you think your teenager felt about the experience?
➤ In what other ways do you help your teenager feel secure?
➤ On a scale of 1 (low) to 10 (high), how would your teenager gauge the need to feel secure?

Acceptance—Isn't it awesome to know God loves us—warts and all? Teenagers want that same kind of acceptance, no matter what flaws they see in their lives. Parents can be open and accepting by focusing on the best rather than the worst they see in their teenager. That doesn't mean you ignore inappropriate behavior or faults that need correcting, but you can accept your teenager as God's creation without approving of their behavior.

Daniel is emerging from two years of defiant behavior that strained his relationship with his family. "I did some really stupid things, Rodney—things I wish I could take back. But every time I walked in that house, I knew Mom and Dad would be there waiting to accept me back. Sometimes, I felt so guilty, but I would go home anyway because I knew they would be there."

Many times, intelligent, wholesome teenagers tell me, "Mom likes my sister more," or, "My dad thinks I'm a geek just because I don't want to play football like my brother." The parents of these teenagers defensively complain, "I love all my children equally." Of course, parents believe that, but we, as parents, respond differently to our children because they have different personalities, abilities, and desires. Body language, tone of voice, and even simple remarks let our young people know whether we accept or reject them. Remember: comparison is the enemy of acceptance.

» Describe the last time you showed your teenager acceptance.
» How did you feel about the experience?
» How do you think your teenager felt about the experience?
» In what other ways do you accept your teenager?
» On a scale of 1 (low) to 10 (high), how would your teenager gauge the need to be accepted?

Loved—Parents offer their teenagers no greater security than the security found in unconditional love. This is love that has no "if onlys": "If only you kept your room clean, I would love you." "If only you would dress like a normal person. . . ." "If only you wouldn't smart-mouth me. . . ." This love looks behind the action to the teenager and says, "I'm still going to love you." This love demands nothing in return. Unconditional love is a conscious choice to love the person no matter what the deed. Many teenagers feel great pressure to achieve in order to earn their parents' love.

I had a girl approach me after she heard me speak in Tampa, Florida. She said, "Rodney, I have been an average student most of my life. I have always felt pressured by my dad to make perfect grades since he was the valedictorian at his high school. Last semester, I went to a tutor before and after school to help me pull up my grades. I even did extra credit when I didn't really have to. Recently, I brought home the best report card I have ever received. I made all As and one B. I couldn't wait to show my dad, thinking he would be so proud. When I showed him my report card, all he said to me was, 'That's great honey, but we need to do something about this B.'" As you can imagine, this young lady was devastated. I believe it's all right to expect the best from your kids; just don't demand perfection.

Unconditional love can also be demonstrated with appropriate affection. Teenagers don't make it easy to show them outward affection. Hugs seem so childish, but a pat on the back, a chuck on the arm, a high five, or a fist bump often say more than words. We've become so frightened in this day of abuse and inappropriate touch that we forget the value of touching.

One of the rituals we have had in our home for years is the foot rub and back rub. Of course, it's always nice to be on the recipient side of a good massage. However, giving this kind of undivided attention is a great way to express your love and affection to your kids; it also provides great moments of conversation.

» Describe the last time you showed your teenager unconditional love.
» How did you feel about the experience?
» How do you think your teenager felt about the experience?

➤ In what other ways do you show unconditional love to your teenager?

➤ On a scale of 1 (low) to 10 (high), how would your teenager gauge the need to be loved unconditionally?

WHAT LIES AHEAD

Do you see how important these five basic gauges are in measuring the needs of teenagers? Perhaps you wonder how you can figure out which needs your teenager has. The following Needs Evaluation is a tool to help you. Show it to your teenager and ask him or her to complete the evaluation. You will also find other ideas for learning your teenager's basic needs in the next three chapters. You will discover what happens when needs are met and what can occur when needs are ignored by parents.

• •

NEEDS EVALUATION

The purpose of this evaluation is to determine what needs you have in your life. Your parent is trying to understand ways to better understand what is most important and meaningful to you in how they show love and support. This evaluation can help. Since there are no right or wrong answers, select a phrase that best represents how you feel about the need in your life. If you don't want to do the evaluation at this time, tell your parent. This is only a tool to help grow your relationship. Even if you don't write down your answers, you might want to look through the statements and mentally check off those you feel you need. Later, you might discuss some of the ideas with your parent.

The basic needs are:

To be	Noticed
To receive	Encouragement
To receive	Empathy
To receive	Direction
To receive	Security

NOTICED

1) I receive focused attention from my family:

Most of the time	some of the time	once in a while	none of the time

2) I am respected for my opinions and ideas as well as in
   my privacy:

Most of the time	some of the time	once in a while	none of the time

3) I am valued as someone special:

Most of the time	some of the time	once in a while	none of the time

4) I am appreciated when I do a job well:

Most of the time	some of the time	once in a while	none of the time

ENCOURAGEMENT

5) I am nurtured or encouraged to reach for my dreams:

Most of the time	some of the time	once in a while	none of the time

6) I am supported when I feel like giving up:

Most of the time	some of the time	once in a while	none of the time

EMPATHY

7) I receive comfort when I experience pain, sorrow,
   despair, or disappointment:

Most of the time	some of the time	once in a while	none of the time

DIRECTION

8) I feel a sense of significance and purpose in my life:

Most of the time	some of the time	once in a while	none of the time

SECURITY

9) I feel physically safe, in addition to feeling that my family is intact and secure:

Most of the time	some of the time	once in a while	none of the time

10) I feel accepted regardless of my flaws and mistakes:

Most of the time	some of the time	once in a while	none of the time

11) I feel loved to matter what I do:

Most of the time	some of the time	once in a while	none of the time

CHAPTER 3

WHEN NEEDS ARE MET

Meeting needs in a positive, healthy manner is the key to motivating teenagers to act in constructive, responsible, and appropriate ways. My parents raised four boys. To their credit, all four of us are serving the Lord. Even though my parents weren't perfect, they made a positive impact on our lives. If there is one factor that made a difference in our lives, it would be the spiritual and moral foundation my parents established from the very beginning. Proverbs 22:6 (AMP) teaches us, "Train up a child in the way he should go [teaching him to seek God's wisdom and will for his abilities and talents], Even when he is old he will not depart from it."

PARENTS MAKE A DIFFERENCE

While there are many factors that can potentially influence a teenager (peers, culture, education, celebrities, developmental growth, etc.), statistics support the fact that parents are still the single most powerful influence in a young person's life.

• •

MEETING NEEDS IN A POSITIVE, HEALTHY MANNER IS THE KEY TO MOTIVATING TEENAGERS TO ACT IN CONSTRUCTIVE, RESPONSIBLE, AND APPROPRIATE WAYS.

• •

» Positive connections to parents and family members can protect teenagers from the use of cigarettes, drugs, and alcohol, according to a study done by the National Longitudinal Study on Adolescent Health. The study found that "high levels of connectedness to parents and family members" reduced teenagers' distress, thoughts of suicide, and feelings of violence.[10] The researchers also learned that a parental presence in the home, along with shared activities by the teenager and the parents, contributed to many healthy choices by the teenager. Negatives that resulted in high-risk behavior included the following: looking older than the teenager's age, easy access to alcohol or drugs in the home, working twenty or more hours a week, and the loss of hope expressed by the feeling that the teenager would die young.[11]

» Encouragement and praise from parents result in teenagers who are more likely to be empathetic with others. This report

10 Michael D. Resnick et al., "Protecting Adolescents from Harm: Findings from the National Longitudinal Study on Adolescent Health," *Journal of the American Medical Association* 278 (September 10, 1997): 823-32 as reported in "Family and School Support Matter," *Assets,* Search Institute (Winter 1997), 12. And "Factors That Affect Children's Use of Drugs," Family Research Council: In Focus, 1998.

11 Michael D. Resnick, et. al., "Protecting Adolescents from Harm . . ."

for *Family Relations* defined empathy as the ability to think from another's point of view and to understand another's feelings. Girls and older teenagers were more empathetic as a whole. But all teenagers who had positive family experiences were able to relate better to others and had effective communication skills.[12]

» A study reported in the *Journal of Early Adolescence* found that close relationships with parents result in emotionally healthy teenagers. Teenagers chose from three levels of relationships with parents: "individuated," "connected," and "detached." Teenagers with "individuated" relationships felt close to their parents with high feelings of freedom. Most of the youth (71 percent with their mothers and 63 percent with their fathers) chose this option. The second largest group (16 percent with their mothers and 19 percent with their fathers) chose "connected" relationships which showed high levels of closeness but lower feelings of freedom. The final group chose "detached" relationships with high levels of freedom but low levels of family closeness. This final group also scored low on indicators of well-being, including levels of anxiety and self-worth.[13]

In addition to the statistical support, I believe the family that offers unconditional love will be the family who meets the needs of its teenagers. Unconditional love is a conscious decision of the

12 Carolyn S. Henry, David W. Sager, and Scott W. Plunkett, "Adolescents' perceptions of family system characteristics, parent-adolescent dyadic behaviors, adolescent qualities, and adolescent empathy," *Family Relations* 45: 283-92 as reported in "Family and School Support Matter," *Assets*, Search Institute (Winter 1997), 12.

13 Mary E. Delaney, "Across the Transition to Adolescence: Qualities of Parent/Adolescent Relationships and Adjustment," *Journal of Early Adolescence* 16, no. 3 (1996): 274-300 as reported in "Connections to Parents Matter," *Assets*, Search Institute (Summer 1997), 11.

will to love another person despite how that person looks, talks, or acts. Conditional love depends on ifs: "I'll love you *if* you don't embarrass me." "I'll love you *if* you make good grades . . . *if* you pick up your room . . . *if* you speak politely to me . . . *if* you don't cause any trouble."

Both kinds of love can be expressed in gestures, body language, tone of voice, and words. Teenagers quickly pick up on inconsistencies. For example, a parent who expresses "I love you" only in connection with pleasing actions does not love unconditionally. A parent who is warm and caring and shows that in an appropriate way to a teenager in good times and difficult times, when the teenager looks "strange" or "normal" (whatever that is for a teenager), or whether the teenager seeks that love or doesn't know to ask for it, this parent loves unconditionally.

• •

LOVING UNCONDITIONALLY IS NOT EASY. YOU MAY NOT BE ABLE TO DO IT ALL THE TIME, BUT IT IS THE GOAL TO SHOOT FOR.

• •

Most teenagers don't know what to call it, but they know unconditional love when they experience it. It had been a brutal two weeks of up-and-down emotions and crises in Corey's eleventh-grade year. Every day felt like a battlefield between him and his parents. One night at the dinner table, Corey lingered after finishing his meal. Only his mother was left at the table. With no prior discussion, Corey blurted out, "I'm sorry that the last two weeks have been so bad. Sometimes, I don't even feel like

I'm in control of what I do. But I do know that you and Dad will love me no matter what happens." Corey's mom told me later that she's glad she didn't say what was going through her mind: *Don't press your luck*! Instead, she was able to hug him and assure Corey that she and his dad would always love him no matter what.

Unconditional love does not mean that you offer life without boundaries. In fact, boundaries are a positive part of loving unconditionally. Boundaries regulate behavior in positive ways. Researchers have determined that boundaries are the single most important element in keeping teenagers from negative behavior, such as substance abuse and delinquency.[14] Setting boundaries gives your teenager the freedom to operate within an acceptable area of behavior. As that teenager matures, those boundaries expand. Smart parents work on teaching their teenagers how to set their own personal boundaries. When boundaries are combined with unconditional love, teenagers act responsibly and with confidence.

Loving unconditionally is not easy. You may not be able to do it all the time, but it is the goal to shoot for. One reason parents struggle with consistent unconditional love is that they start with the wrong assumptions. Assumptions get you in trouble because you don't look beyond the assumption. The person assumes he knows everything about the situation—that he has an unbiased, perfect perspective. Assumptions begin with a false premise and are usually too broad, too narrow, or too one-sided, making it difficult to discover your teenager's real needs.

---

14 Melissa S. Herman, Sanford M. Dornbush, Michael C. Herron, and Jerald R. Herting, "The Influence of Family Regulation, Connection, and Psychological Autonomy on Six Measures of Adolescent Functioning," *Journal of Adolescent Research* 12:34-37 as reported in *Assets*, Search Institute (Spring 1997), 13.

DON'T ASSUME ANYTHING!

Assumption #1: My teenager seems okay. I must be doing everything right. Many parents refuse to look beyond the surface behavior of their teenagers. As one youth put it, "I don't lie to my folks. I just don't tell them everything." Some teenagers are very good at hiding inappropriate behavior. To the rest of the world, they look and act in acceptable ways. These teenagers are the most likely ones to choose destructive or unhealthy behavior once they leave home—either for college or to live and work on their own.

Assumption #2: My teenager is a mess. I'm a terrible parent. I can't possibly meet this kid's needs. Parents often ask, "How could this happen to my teenager?" While the family plays a major role in the life of a young person, they are not the only influence. Other adults, peers, and social pressures push teenagers into unhealthy actions. Don't beat yourself up. You picked up this book with the intention of finding an answer. Use it as a springboard to a new beginning with your teenager. Chapter 11 deals with healing the hurt that may have been caused by a teenager and/or a parent. You will learn when and how to get professional help or intervention.

• •

DON'T BEAT YOURSELF UP. YOU PICKED UP THIS BOOK WITH THE INTENTION OF FINDING AN ANSWER.

• •

Assumption #3: It's just a phase of adolescence. I made it through my teenage years. Much of a teen's normal behavior appears abnormal to parents. Parents must learn what normal developmental behavior is. Then, as a parent, you'll be in a better position to recognize what behavior comes from the developmental process and what doesn't. Don't hide from the world your teenager lives in. It is much tougher than the world of your adolescence. Today's teenagers are exposed to everything imaginable because of technology: easy access to pornography, drugs, sexual assault, offensive language, dysfunctional adults, and blatant challenges to their values and beliefs—and that's just in their schools and neighborhoods. With tough pressures like these, parents must stay engaged with their teenager's world and their teenager's needs.

A youth minister friend shared a conversation he had with two families from his student ministry. Both families' teenagers continually caused problems by being disruptive, using offensive language, making vulgar remarks and gestures, and defying adults who were their leaders. With both families in the same room, the youth minister stated, "Your teenagers are out of control and have become more than we can handle in our student ministry. They are serving as a distraction to the other students who are trying to grow. We love your students, and we want them here, but we can't have them participate with us at the expense of the other students."

One set of parents took his warning and began to take the important steps toward understanding what core issues were driving their son's negative behavior. They began to address those concerns with their son. Over a period of time, with lots of prayer, tough love, and patience, their teenager began cutting ties with the wrong friends and started reconnecting with the church. He started making an effort to change and grow in his faith. The other family left the meeting, saying, "He'll be okay. It's just a phase he's going through." My friend shared how sad it has been to watch the decline of this young man. Because his parents were afraid or unable to get on the same page to help their son by setting healthy and effective boundaries, consequently, that teenager continued getting into trouble with increasing frequency. He was only fourteen years old.

Assumption #4: It's too late. It's too early. It is never too late to work on any relationship. If you want to restore a relationship with your teenager and try to help that teenager make it into adulthood safely, start today. It requires determination. It may take longer than you expect, but if you start now, you have a chance to rebuild a relationship with your teenager and make a difference in his or her life.

It is never too early. In fact, you have been meeting the needs of your child from the cradle. Some children enter puberty before they actually turn thirteen. These early bloomers are already dealing with needs and issues related to being a teenager. Some parents think that once this child becomes a teenager, they don't need to be as involved as they previously were. The amount of attention and importance of meeting needs does not diminish during the teenage years. Parents must stay engaged.

Assumption #5: My teenager will turn out better than me. We all want a better life and a safer world for our children. Most parents wish they could shield their children from the pain and reality of the world, but they can't. They also can't turn their teenager into someone that the teenager doesn't want to be. You can offer your teenager the opportunities. You can provide encouragement and support. You can wish and dream and hope and pray. But in the end, you can't assume that your teenager will be a better, more talented, or more successful adult than you. Family psychologist John Rosemond states it this way: "It's your job to provide good directions; it's your child's job to follow them."[15]

Assumption #6: I'm (select your problem) a single parent, unemployed, uneducated, an only child, financially strapped, or climbing the corporate ladder, so I don't have the (select your excuse) time, energy, training, money, emotional ability, or patience to determine my teenager's needs and meet them. Parenting is sometimes inconvenient. But parenting can also be a great joy. You took on the task of preparing this person for adulthood. Just because the job of parenting can be hard doesn't mean it's time to stop. You may have to put your needs on hold in order to invest time, energy, and emotions into raising your teenager. (Many of us didn't know we signed up for all this when we first became a parent—but surprise! We did!)

Well, as you can see, there are a lot of assumptions that can be made. You can probably come up with more. The bottom line is don't assume. Instead, discover your teenager's true needs by becoming a Parent Investigator.

• •

THE BOTTOM LINE IS DON'T ASSUME. INSTEAD, DISCOVER YOUR TEENAGER'S TRUE NEEDS BY BECOMING A PARENT INVESTIGATOR.

• •

15 John Rosemond, "Quality of Child-Rearing Provides No Guarantees," *The Atlanta-Journal Constitution*, July 17, 1998, C2.

A PARENT INVESTIGATOR (PI)

Before you jump to false conclusions (Remember: never assume!), let me explain what I mean about being a parent investigator. First of all, I'm not talking about pulling out your 007 secret identity. This is not about the bad guys against the good guys. I'm not suggesting you become a spy; that violates the privacy and personhood of your teenager. Neither do you have to be a bloodhound sniffing into others' business. I want you to stay focused on learning the needs of your teenager, so you can meet those needs.

An investigator is someone who observes what is going on, takes all the clues, and puts them into place. An investigator inquires about the situation, gathering details to figure out the bigger picture. As a PI, I encourage you to observe and inquire to get to the need. You don't have to be a snoop, but you must be a keen observer who recognizes the signals that indicate trouble. You are looking for clues—a drastic change in behavior, suddenly becoming secretive, different sleeping or eating habits, increasing defiance, withdrawal, or problems at school—that show a pattern. You can be observant and ask questions without prying.

Only if you determine a consistent pattern of negative behavior should you be more aggressive. When you become alarmed about the health or well-being of your teenager, that is the time to act. Be prepared, however, to deal with the consequences. For example, if you search your teenager's room for drugs, know what you are going to do if you find them. Will you confront your teenager, use intervention to get your teenager into a drug rehabilitation program, or send your teenager to a professional counselor?

Test your PI skills in the following scenarios.

An excited fifteen-year-old girl named Shannon laid a sheet of paper down in front of her dad who was working at his computer. "If you'll sign this, I can try out for the high school soccer team." Her dad looked at the paper and replied:

Response #1

"You haven't played soccer since the eighth grade. I always thought you were really good, so tell me why the renewed interest?" As Shannon shared her desire to play again, she and her dad worked out how she would get home from practices, how she could balance practice with her homework, and when the different games were. As he handed Shannon the signed paper, her dad smiled, "I know you'll make the team. It'll be great watching you play again."

Response #2

"When do you expect to have time for soccer? And who do you think can keep up with getting you home from all those practices? Your mom and I are maxed out right now! I bet you drop out like you did a couple of years ago." After he signed the paper, he stated gruffly, "Don't let this interfere with your regular responsibilities or your homework." Shannon crumpled up the paper as she walked out of the room.

Response #3

"I'll look at it later. I've got to get this computer glitch worked out."

Granted, teenagers do not always pick the best times to talk, to ask questions, or to seek help. They have a built-in radar that tells them the most annoying time to interrupt. When you're ready to talk, they are either too busy or gone. But even assuming that Shannon's dad was busy and her interruption was inconvenient, let's evaluate the different responses to see how Shannon's needs were met.

First, what physical and emotional needs did Shannon have when she showed her dad the paper?

Response #1 Result

Based on the time her father took and the words he said, Shannon walked away feeling pretty good about herself and her decision to try out for the soccer team. Her dad seemed genuinely interested in knowing what was going on in her life.

His encouragement and support made her feel like she could make the team and play with confidence.

If you were Shannon, what would you be thinking as you walked away?

What would you be feeling?

How might you behave based on these thoughts and feelings?

Response #2 Result

Her father's words deflated Shannon's enthusiasm. Maybe she had caught him at a bad time, but lately, he'd been on her about one thing after another. He never listened to what she had to say. She should have known he wouldn't care. Why make an effort to do anything if no one cares?

What would you be thinking as you walked away?

What would you be feeling?

How might you behave based on these thoughts and feelings? Why do you think Shannon crumpled up the signed form?

Response #3 Result

Shannon waited a couple of minutes to see if her dad would look up from the computer. When he didn't, she turned and went back to her room. After finishing her math, she went back to see if her dad had signed the form. She didn't see it on his desk. When she started looking for it, her dad yelled at her. Shannon returned to her bedroom, knowing she'd never see the form before tomorrow's deadline.

If you were Shannon, what would you be thinking as you walked away?

What would you be feeling?

How might you behave based on these thoughts and feelings?

Psychologists, educators, and others recognize the connection between thinking, feeling, behaving, and needs. The process of thinking, feeling, and behaving is how we get our needs met. If you look beyond the behavior to the thoughts and feelings that precede that behavior, you can usually figure out the need involved. These simple scenarios demonstrate this relationship between needs and the resulting behavior. When Shannon's needs were met, she had healthy thoughts that made her feel good, and she reacted positively. When Shannon's needs were not met, her negative thoughts made her feel lousy, and she reacted by getting angry, by feeling ignored, and by resenting her dad. To her, indifference (response 3) was the same as rejection.

A TEEN'S PERSPECTIVE

Let's take a look at what thoughts, feelings, and behavior means for teenagers.

I Am What I Feel!

Dr. Mary Pipher, in *Reviving Ophelia*, a revealing study of adolescent girls, reminds us that feelings dominate the thought patterns of teenagers. Teenage girls are especially vulnerable to "emotional reasoning, which is the belief that if you feel something is true, it must be true."[16] If a teenager feels stupid, she or he must be stupid. Teenagers further tend to expand the "truth" to relate to a period of time that goes beyond the present. If a teenager feels ignored by a parent, she believes her parent will ignore her forever. Feeling and thinking become intertwined in such a way that teenagers often can't distinguish the two.

Young teenagers' feelings are intensified by raging hormones and other developmental changes. Most high school students are acquiring the mental ability and the emotional stability to separate feelings from thoughts. To help your teenager separate thinking from feeling, ask questions like, "How do you feel about this situation?" and "What do you think about this situation?" Have them calculate the level or degree of their emotions. For example, if your teenager says, "I hate Martha!" You might ask, "How much do you hate her? Lots? A little? In between? On a scale of one to ten, where's your hate?" Sometimes helping a teenager evaluate the feelings and judge the intensity defuses the emotion and makes it more manageable for the teenager.

---

16 Mary Pipher, *Reviving Ophelia: Saving the Selves of Adolescent Girls* (New York, NY: Ballentine Books, 1994) 60.

• •

FEELING AND THINKING BECOME INTERTWINED IN SUCH A WAY THAT TEENAGERS OFTEN CAN'T DISTINGUISH THE TWO.

• •

Feelings can overpower thinking.

Daniel Goleman, in his book *Emotional Intelligence*, suggests that people are made up with two minds—one that thinks and one that feels. He also explains a process that you might have noticed with your teenager or even yourself:

The emotional mind is far quicker than the rational mind, springing into action without pausing even a moment to consider what it is doing. Its quickness precludes the deliberate, analytic reflection that is the hallmark of the thinking mind. . . . When the dust settles, or even in mid-response, we find ourselves thinking, "What did I do that for?"—a sign that the rational mind is awakening to the moment, but not with the rapidity of the emotional mind.[17]

Anyone who has ever ended up in an argument with a teenager will recognize the progression of skipping over the thinking process and responding immediately from a feeling perspective— then wondering later, *How did that happen? I used to be able to control my temper better than that!* For the teenager, the emotional mind or feeling part often operates first, resulting in more than one occasion where the teenager can truthfully say, "I don't know why I did that."

---

17 Daniel Goleman, *Emotional Intelligence* (New York, NY: Bantam Books, 1995), 291-92.

Please Refill My Emotional Tank

Ross Campbell, in *How to Really Love Your Teenager*, talks about everyone, especially teenagers, having an emotional tank. When that emotional tank is full, needs are being met. A teenager with a full emotional tank ventures into the world to interact in positive, healthy ways. As the teenager expresses his independence by going places on his own, by following his peers, by testing the rules and boundaries, his emotional tank empties. If the teenager cannot refill that emotional tank at home, he will look for another filling station.

• •

FOR THE TEENAGER, THE EMOTIONAL MIND OR FEELING PART OFTEN OPERATES FIRST, RESULTING IN MORE THAN ONE OCCASION WHERE THE TEENAGER CAN TRUTHFULLY SAY, "I DON'T KNOW WHY I DID THAT."

• •

A PI who is paying attention will notice that the emotional tank is getting empty and start to do things to refill the tank—spend time with the teenager, offer praise and encouragement for jobs well done, express love and support through notes, and so on. With a refilled tank, the teenager, once again, handles life with healthy behavior. Campbell emphasizes the importance of this refilling:

➤ Teenagers need an ample amount of emotional nurturance if they are to function at their best and grow to be their best.

➤ They desperately need full emotional tanks in order to feel the security and self-confidence they must have to cope with peer pressure and other demands from youth culture. Without this confidence, teenagers tend to succumb to peer pressure and experience difficulty in upholding wholesome, ethical values.

➤ The emotional refilling is crucial because while it is taking place, it is possible to keep open lines of communication between parents and teenagers.[18]

I'm Not Like You

Parents often project what they think their teenagers need rather than taking the time to discover a teenager's real needs. An effective PI will keep observing and inquiring until that parent knows what the teenager needs.

How a teenager wants a need met may be different from how the parent meets that need. Once again, the wise PI tests the gauges to see which are indicating a problem. If the teenager doesn't respond to what the parent does to meet that need, the parent must try a different approach. Sometimes a parent must resort to trial and error to find what works best with that particular teenager.

---

18 Ross Campbell, *How to Really Love Your Teenager* (Wheaton, IL: Victor Books, 1981), 29-30.

HOW EMOTIONAL GAUGES WORK

While understanding the thinking, feeling, behaving process may help a parent define the need, it's not an exact science.

Gauges	Indicates Constructive Thinking	Indicates Favorable Feelings	Results in Appropriate Behaviors
Noticed	My dad pays attention to me.	Valued as a person	shows kindness to others
Encouragement	My family supports my efforts.	Confidence	works to complete a task
Empathy	My mom cares when I hurt.	Assurance	develops caring relationships with others
Direction	I receive praise for my actions.	Significant	accepts leadership responsibilities
Security	I feel accepted no matter what I do.	Loved	treats others politely

This chart gives you a visual of how the process ought to work. These are examples of how the thinking, feeling, behaving process builds off of needs. There are unlimited combinations of feelings and thoughts and behaviors, but you can see the vital relationship between this process and meeting needs. So how are you going to determine your teenager's needs? By becoming a gauge reader.

LEARN TO BE A GAUGE READER

Remember that the gauges indicate what is going on in the life of your teenager. Here is a checklist of ways to become an effective gauge reader.

Show your teenager the Needs Evaluation at the end of chapter 2. Explain why you are asking your teenager to complete this evaluation. Encourage your teenager to mark each need honestly. Ask your teenager to circle their top three needs by numbering those from one to three.

» Were you aware of the needs your teenager selected?
» What behaviors in the past few months have you noticed that could be linked to the top needs marked by your teenager?

If you don't think your teenager will do the evaluation, talk with your teenager. Explain that you are trying to become a better parent. Share a few ideas about emotional needs. Ask a couple of questions like these to get the discussion started. Then, listen:

» Tell me about a time when you felt I was unfair or uncaring.
» How did you feel about my failure to listen?
» When you are with your friends, how do you feel?
» When you are with our family, how do you feel?
» What is the most difficult part of being a member of this family?

These are tough questions but encourage honesty. Pay attention to what is not said. Remember: you are listening to discover—not to defend.

» Become an expert on your teenager. Observe what event, action, or response triggers negative behavior. Back away from the teen's behavior and try to discover the feelings and thoughts that led to the behavior. Watch the people your teen wants to be with. What do they offer that attracts your teen? You are trying to change the source of the behavior—not simply correct the behavior. You may want to keep a journal or notebook to see if there is a pattern of behavior. You are not looking at individual episodes of wrong behavior but for the pattern.

➤➤ Ask for another person's perspective. Day-to-day parenting makes it difficult to get a clear perspective. Explain your desire to be a better parent to a trusted person who is around your teenager. This might be a youth minister, a neighbor, a school counselor, a coach, or a parent of your teen's best friend. Discuss which needs this person sees in your teenager's life.

• •

WHEN ALL ELSE FAILS, USE TRIAL AND ERROR. DON'T GET DISCOURAGED IF YOU DON'T SEE A CHANGE. YOUR GOAL IS TO IDENTIFY AND MEET YOUR TEENAGER'S NEEDS.

• •

➤➤ Talk with other parents of teenagers. Find out what behaviors they see in their teenagers and how these behaviors develop. Ask what needs they recognize most often in their teenagers. Other parents can not only help you distinguish between normal and abnormal behavior, but they can also encourage and support you as you try to keep your teen's emotional gauges in balance.

➤ When all else fails, use trial and error. Work through the emotional gauges one at a time. As you do specific things, note responses or changes in your teen's behavior. This process takes time. Don't get discouraged if you don't see a change. Your goal is to identify and meet your teenager's needs.

Keep these gauge reader ideas in mind as we now look at why teenagers experience unmet needs.

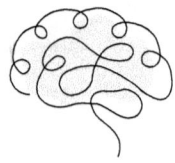

CHAPTER 4

WHEN NEEDS AREN'T MET

When a teenager doesn't receive appreciation, security, comfort, or whatever that teenager needs at home, he or she seeks an alternate source. That other source may be a group that embraces them and accepts them for who he or she is. But what if this accepting, new group embraces wrong beliefs and values or participates in negative or destructive actions: vandalism, alcohol and drug abuse, sexual promiscuity, parental defiance, or unacceptable language?

Why do teenagers get involved with these groups? The answer is simple but painful. Hurting teenagers, who are so absorbed in getting their unmet needs satisfied, willingly compromise personal morals and convictions to be accepted, to feel approval, and to gain the attention often denied by their families. As Walt Mueller, founder of the Center for Parent/Youth

Understanding, says, "If we choose not to mold and shape our children, someone else will."[19]

• •

HURTING TEENAGERS, WHO ARE SO ABSORBED IN GETTING THEIR UNMET NEEDS SATISFIED, WILLINGLY COMPROMISE PERSONAL MORALS AND CONVICTIONS TO BE ACCEPTED, TO FEEL APPROVAL, AND TO GAIN THE ATTENTION OFTEN DENIED BY THEIR FAMILIES.

• •

MASKS TEENS WEAR

When needs go unmet, teenagers may put on a mask to hide their feelings. These masks are usually chosen unconsciously, but they express the feelings and thoughts of the teenager. The masks might look different on different teenagers, but these are the ones I see most often.

Penny the Perfectionist

Teenagers put on this mask to prove themselves to their parents. Wearing this mask, the teenager assumes perfectionist tendencies, obsessive-compulsive work, or dissatisfaction with personal accomplishments. This mask covers up the unmet needs for acceptance, unconditional love, and appreciation.

Susan gets so tense before a test that she becomes physically ill. Once the test is over, she talks about what she missed and what she should have written or done. She's not even happy if the test

---

19 Walt Mueller, "Virtual Parenting," *Living with Teenagers*, September 1998, 10.

comes back with a good grade. Susan carries this tendency for perfection into the way she prepares reports, reworking them several times until the report must be turned in.

Explosive Emily

This teenager is a normal person who usually hides or keeps any feelings of pain, hurt, or rejection to herself for as long as possible. Then one day, something triggers that pain, and she explodes like a volcano, spewing angry words and negative behavior over anyone unfortunate enough to be nearby. This teenager doesn't wake up one morning and decide, *Today's the day I'm going to lose it.* The explosion just happens. Teenagers in dysfunctional homes or abusive situations may wear this mask, although other situations can cause the deep feelings of pain and rejection. This mask covers up unmet needs for comfort, respect, love, and attention.

Marcia had been suspended from school for kicking a teacher and causing a general melee in class one day. Her excuse, "I hate algebra. I don't understand it. I don't see why I need it. I hate school!" didn't add up for Pat Lacey, another of Marcia's teachers. Later that summer at youth camp, Marcia told Mrs. Lacey, a camp counselor, that she had been raped by three boys late one afternoon after school under the stairs. They threatened her life if she told on them. The rape took place two months prior to Marcia attacking her teacher.

Directionless Doug

This teenager lacks direction or purpose. He prefers to hang out in his room and doesn't care about school, sports, or any other activities. His friends change quickly; in fact, he may not have any friends. His social skills are nil. When other youths try to include him in their conversation, he shuffles his feet and eventually walks away from the group. If you ask Doug what's happening in his life, he replies, "Nothing." If you ask Doug what his interests are, he replies, "Nothing." This mask covers up the unmet needs of direction and purpose, support, and encouragement.

Confrontational Chris

This teenager loves to pick a fight. He's known for attacking others verbally. Debates with this teenager usually turn into arguments. In some instances, arguments may even end in physical confrontations. This teenager may resort to gangs or activist groups as an expression of his anger and hostility. This mask covers up the unmet needs for encouragement, feeling valued and noticed, comfort, and love.

Promiscuous Pete

This teenager chooses sex as a substitute for love. For guys, this can become a sexual contest taken to extremes. For girls, it can be a desire to belong to somebody—anybody. Walt Mueller explains this mask this way:

> *Research has shown that teens will often use sex as a means to express and satisfy emotional and interpersonal needs that have little or nothing to do with sex. Sexual intercourse becomes a coping mechanism to deal with the absence of love and affection at home and a groping mechanism as they grasp at any experience that might fill that void.*[20]

This mask covers up the unmet needs for love and affection, nurturing, and support.

---

20 Walt Mueller, "Rediscovering Love," *Living with Teenagers*, February 1998, 9.

Jill the Joker

This teenager makes others laugh to get attention. At first, the behavior is funny, but the constant jokes at inappropriate times and the demand for the spotlight all the time make it difficult to tolerate this teenager for long. This teenager's parents never look beneath the humor to see the insecurity they feel. This mask covers up the unmet needs for attention, respect, value, and appreciation.

Sally Secluded

This teenager uses her mask to withdraw from the world. She sees herself as a victim of life. Everything that happens to her is intentional. Every criticism, correction, or suggestion was spoken to hurt her feelings. She trusts no one. She comes home from school and goes into her cave (room). This teenager may not attempt anything like a sport or going to camp or studying a tough subject because she believes she will fail. She believes she is inferior because she feels inferior. (Remember: feelings are reality to many teenagers.)

Nate's parents tend to minimize honor and respect in their home based on how they talk down to each other, and they treat Nate with the same lack of respect. Nate can't remember his dad ever praising any activity Nate did. However, Nate can remember the exact critical words his dad said to him about how he looked one day. Nate prefers hanging out in his bedroom to the family room. This mask covers up the unmet needs for respect, appreciation, security, significance, and purpose.

Frank the Follower

A teenager wearing this mask is easily swayed by the crowd. Even though the crowd may change (school, church, ball team, etc.), this teenager goes along with whatever they decide to do—good or bad. This mask covers up the unmet needs of acceptance, attention, value as a person, and love.

Blaine's parents were surprised one night when they answered the doorbell and saw Blaine standing there with a policeman. The officer had brought her home from a party after neighbors called the police because of the rowdy teenagers. Blaine was too drunk to drive. Her parents didn't even know she drank.

UNMASKING THE NEEDS

Teenagers choose these alternate behaviors to achieve two goals: One goal is to avoid the pain of not having a need met. The other is to feel better, connected, loved, or accepted by anyone, anywhere. That's the bottom line—to avoid the pain and to feel connected.

Red Alert Gauges	Red Alert Thinking	Red Alert Feelings	Red Alert Behaviors
Unnoticed	My dad doesn't care what I do.	anxious	addictions
Discouraged	I always do something wrong.	Self-doubt	fails to complete tasks
Ignored	No one cares when I hurt.	Empty and alone	withdrawal
Rejected	I don't do anything worthwhile.	Insignificant	can't make friends
Insecure	I never feel accepted.	Unloved	easily angered

Just as reading the gauges tells you when your teenager's emotional tank is full, a teenager's negative behavior means you need to look at the gauges and realize that the emotional tank is either empty or has been refilled by others who do not have the best interest of your teenager in mind. Why are some parents ineffective at meeting their teenager's needs?

• •

A TEENAGER'S NEGATIVE BEHAVIOR MEANS YOU NEED TO LOOK AT THE GAUGES AND REALIZE THAT THE EMOTIONAL TANK IS EITHER EMPTY OR HAS BEEN REFILLED BY OTHERS WHO DO NOT HAVE THE BEST INTEREST OF YOUR TEENAGER IN MIND.

• •

Sometimes, it's a matter of ineffective roles, unusual stress, or fatherless homes.

INEFFECTIVE PARENTAL ROLES

Parents can damage their relationship with their teenagers by assuming ineffective roles. Often these roles were modeled by the grandparents, so the parents don't know how harmful these roles could be. Other roles may be assumed as a convenience or to hide a parent's own frustration, lack of unmet needs, or feelings of inadequacy. The following checklist may help you discover which ineffective role you might play.

The Nag
» Are you constantly asking your teenager to do a task without a successful response?

➤ Does the teenager's lack of response make you angry?

➤ Is it easier to nag than do it yourself?

➤ Do you nag your teenager about more than one activity or task at a time?

This parent substitutes nagging for communication. One way to stop playing this role is to figure out why the teenager responds with procrastination. (If the parent models procrastination, though, don't be surprised if the teenager just follows the example.) Another way to stop playing the nag's role is to set a time limit on the task to be completed: "The grass needs to be cut by Friday evening." Restate the time frame once: "Today is Thursday. Don't forget to cut the grass by tomorrow night." If there is still no response, the nag can let the request go and live with the consequences, find someone else to do it, or do the task personally. Nagging can be habit-forming.

The Pretender

➤ Have you been hurt in the past by your teenager's actions or words?

➤ Do you hide the hurt and decide not to deal with it?

➤ Do you pretend that nothing's wrong between your teenager and you?

➤ When your teenager does something that is offensive or hurts your feelings, do you escape in your home office, suffer in silence, or pout?

This parent looks composed on the outside but is much like the Explosive Emily mask worn by the teenager. Holding in the hurt, anger, and frustration may cover up hurt feelings, but the potential for anger lies near the surface. The parent in this role can't see their teenager's unmet needs through the veil of suffering sainthood. However, any parent in this situation must first determine what sets off the feelings of hurt or pain they are experiencing in their own life. Once those feelings are identified, then the parent should share that pain with another adult friend who can comfort and listen.

One way to quit playing this role of the pretender is for the parent to honestly recognize their unwillingness to confront the teenager after the offense. Once this parent recognizes their own emotions and lets their teenager know how they are affected, the parent can look more accurately at their teen's negative behavior and what needs that are being neglected in their teen's life.

The Escape Artist

➤ Do you blame others for your parenting problems?

➤ Are the problems with your teenager someone else's fault?

➤ Do you use put-downs and teasing when you talk to your teenager?

➤ Do you use derogatory words to describe your teenager to others?

Like an escape artist who sneaks out the back door to keep from being seen, the parent usually hides behind this role to avoid responsibility. This parent relates to the teenager by casting blame on others, even blaming the teenager. To stop playing this role, the parent must act like an adult and accept responsibility.

If the parent has continually blamed the teenager for the teenager's problems, the parent may need to mend the relationship by offering a sincere apology to the teenager and asking for forgiveness.

The Spy

» Do you snoop in your teenager's room and regularly go through clothing pockets (not clothes for the washing machine—but hanging clothes)?

» Do you listen in on your teenager's telephone conversations?

» Do you grill the teenager about where he went, whom he was with, and what happened?

» Do you distrust your teenager?

The spy or paranoid parent does more damage to the relationship with the teenager than any other ineffective parental role.

Teenagers can tell when a parent snoops, and they know snooping comes from a lack of trust. By nature, teenagers become more secretive as they seek independence from family. But a teenager who has a spy for a parent will grow even more careful and mysterious. Many times, paranoid parents drive their teenagers away.

This parent usually doesn't think about how he will react if he finds evidence to back up his suspicions. Should the parent confront the teenager and admit her spying or do nothing and worry over what has been discovered? This parent must stop playing this role and restore strong, open communication lines with the teenager. To begin the process of restoration, the spy might make a list of fears and share a few of these with the teenager. This parent should remember to look for a pattern of behavior with supporting signs before spying.

The Drill Sergeant

» Does your communication come in the form of orders or instructions?

» Are you used to being in charge of the situation?

» Do you feel like you have all the answers for your teenager's problems?

» Do you expect your teenager to follow your orders without any feedback?

» Do you always have a plan?

This role involves power. Frequently this parent transfers the position of power she has at the office to the home, or the parent may feel helpless at the office, so he uses his home to express his power. This parent won't be able to recognize a teenager's needs until he is willing to step down from his position of power.

To quit the drill sergeant role, this parent must surrender some power and freedom to the teenager, especially as the teenager gets older and learns to make decisions on his or her own. The drill sergeant can begin to share the power by offering the teenager two or three options instead of telling him or her what to do. He also can strengthen his relationship with his teenager by sharing times when he feels vulnerable.

The MIA (Missing in Attention)

» Do you find it easier to stay out of your teenager's life?

» Do you prefer not to know what's happening?

» Do you believe that your teenager is totally responsible for himself?

» Are you too busy to attend your teenager's games or performances, go to the teenager's school for conferences, or work with your teenager on projects or personal interests?

This parent is missing in attention, being too busy or preoccupied to pay attention to his teenager. Many parents at this time in their lives are at the peaks of their careers and feel compelled to work long hours, leaving little time for family, much less for a teenager. A teenager's busy schedule complicates this relationship. Sometimes the MIA may not be so busy but is unwilling to deal with the world of his teenager. The indifferent parent refuses to get involved with the teenager. Some parents accept the MIA role because they have no idea how to relate to a teenager.

To stop playing this role, the parent must get involved in the teenager's life by giving that teenager focused attention on a regular basis. This parent may have to make hard choices between career and family.

Did you recognize yourself playing any of these roles? Perhaps you know of other roles parents use to hide their insecurities and their personal shortcomings. Parents can keep playing the roles, or they can choose to stop. Once a parent understands how roles prevent a parent from recognizing and meeting a teenager's needs, then that parent can stop playing the role and look beyond the teenager's surface behavior to determine real needs.

• •

ONCE A PARENT UNDERSTANDS HOW ROLES PREVENT THEM FROM RECOGNIZING AND MEETING A TEENAGER'S NEEDS, THEN THAT PARENT CAN STOP PLAYING THE ROLE AND LOOK BEYOND THE TEENAGER'S SURFACE BEHAVIOR TO DETERMINE REAL NEEDS.

• •

STRESSED OUT

Occasionally, all parents must deal with heavy stress. Parents in this situation may feel guilty for not meeting their teenager's needs. Some stress is inevitable in life, but too much stress can harm or even paralyze relationships. Take a look at how much stress has occurred in your life over the past twelve months using this adapted version of the Holmes-Rahe scale developed by Drs. Thomas Holmes and Richard H. Rahe at the University of Washington Medical School.

- ❏ death of a spouse, 100
- ❏ divorce, 73
- ❏ marital separation, 65
- ❏ jail term, 63
- ❏ death of a close family member, 63
- ❏ personal injury or illness, 53
- ❏ marriage, 50
- ❏ fired from work, 47
- ❏ reconciliation with mate, 45
- ❏ change in family member's health, 44
- ❏ sexual difficulties, 39
- ❏ addition to the family, 39
- ❏ change in financial status 38
- ❏ death of a close friend, 37
- ❏ change in line of work, 36
- ❏ change in number of marital arguments, 35
- ❏ debt over $10,000, 31
- ❏ change in work responsibilities, 29
- ❏ son or daughter leaving home, 29
- ❏ trouble with in-laws, 31

- ❏ outstanding personal achievement, 28
- ❏ trouble with boss, 23
- ❏ change in work hours, conditions, 20
- ❏ change in residence, 20
- ❏ change in schools, 20
- ❏ debt under $10,000, 17
- ❏ change in sleeping habits, 16
- ❏ change in eating habits, 15
- ❏ vacation, 13
- ❏ Christmas season, 12

Total the points for each stress factor you checked. Parents with a score of 150 or less are less likely to feel pulled in several different directions. Parents with a score of 150 to 300 have a moderate amount of stress that may be taking its toll on time and energy. Scores of over 300 mean a family has excessive stress. Symptoms of a family operating under excessive stress may include:

» A general feeling of urgency.

» Sharp words, misunderstandings, and an underlying tension among family members.

» A desire to escape either to the bedroom, the car, the office, or almost anywhere.

» Feeling frustrated for not being "caught up" with regular responsibilities.

» Not having time for regular personal care.

» Feeling guilty for not taking care of everyone in the family.

The higher the stress, the greater the chances of a family malfunctioning. Here are several ideas to help bring down the levels of stress:

» Identify what causes the stress.

» Work with the family to find solutions for the stress.

» Allow the teenager to take on some responsibility, if possible.

» Involve other people who can help with the workload or offer perspective.
» Make a list of what needs to be done to diminish the stress; then, work through the list.
» Revise the chores.
» Focus on the strengths of your family.
» Find someone outside the family who can listen to your frustration.

FATHERLESS HOMES

Over and over, one thing I consistently hear from teenagers who are hurting is the loss they feel from a lack of a dad in the home. Before going any further, let me state how much I appreciate single-parent moms who provide excellent homes for their teenagers and who are meeting their teenagers' needs to the best of their ability. But I believe these mothers will agree with me that not having a dad or father figure in the home is a great loss.

Here are some of the painful statistics:

» 43% of U.S. children live without their father.
» 70% of youths in state-operated institutions come from fatherless homes—9 times the average.
» Daughters of single parents without a Father involved are 53% more likely to marry as teenagers, 711% more likely to have children as teenagers, 164% more likely to have a pre-marital birth and 92% more likely to get divorced themselves.
» 71% of high school dropouts come from fatherless homes—9 times the average.

» 90% of homeless and runaway children are from fatherless homes.

» 75% of all adolescent patients in chemical abuse centers come from fatherless homes—10 times the average.[21]

Walt Mueller, in his book *Understanding Today's Youth Culture*, identified the fatherless home as one of the greatest disruptions in the lives of teenagers:

We now know that father absence is the greatest variable in the present and future well-being of children and teens. Children who grow through the difficult, challenging, and formative years of adolescence without their dads have a greater risk of suffering from emotional and behavioral problems such as sexual promiscuity, premarital teen pregnancy, substance abuse, depression, suicide, lower academic performance, dropping out of school, intimacy dysfunction, divorce, and poverty.[22]

There is hope as fathers are coming together, reclaiming their roles, and stepping up to be a part of their children's lives. Some single-parent moms have been able to work through their churches or community groups to find male mentors for their sons and daughters. This remains a serious problem for the American family.

IDENTIFYING BEHAVIORS AND NEEDS

Identify the specific behaviors you see in your teenager. Use the NEEDS gauges listed in chapter 2 or the Needs Evaluation filled

---

21 "Research and Statistics," *Rochester Area Fatherhood Network*, http://www.rochesterareafatherhoodnetwork.org/statistics.

22 Walt Mueller, *Understanding Today's Youth Culture* (Wheaton, IL: Tyndale House, 1994), 4.

out by your teen to determine which of his or her needs is going unmet. Consider the need from the teenager's point of view.

>> What thoughts and feelings has the teenager experienced because of the unmet need?
>> What feelings might the teenager still feel?
>> How can you make the situation better, improve the relationship, or meet the unmet need? List specific actions you can take.

Remember that God is a God of both mercy and grace. Ask Him to go before you as you talk with your teenager about your desire to correct the unmet needs. Ask God to bring healing to you and your teenager.

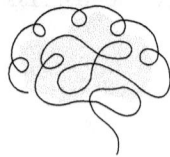

CHAPTER 5

TEENS AND RELATIONSHIPS

t's been said, "Parenting is simple but not easy." Just about the time you've figured out how to relate to an energetic twelve-year-old, you run into the wall of silence that defines a thirteen-year-old. Learning what your teenager's emotional needs are can be challenging. You can't operate on autopilot and assume your teenager's gauges indicate a full emotional tank. You are always a parent-in-training.

INTENSE NEEDS, INTENSE RELATIONSHIPS

For a teenager, the craving for fulfilled needs is intense. Teenagers spend their teen years trying to answer one question: who am I? It is not an easy question. There are no easy answers. Les Parrott explains how the search for identity works:

Somewhere between twelve and twenty years of age adolescents are forced to choose once and for all what their identity is to be.

It is a formidable task. Uncertain which of their mixed emotions are really their true feelings, they are pushed to make up their minds. Their confusion is complicated further when they begin to guess what others, whose opinions they care about, want them to be. . . . This not only creates tension in the life of the teenager, but also in the teenager's relationships, especially those with parents.[23]

• •

WE ARE ALWAYS PARENTS-IN-TRAINING.

• •

Normal teenage development intensifies a teenager's needs. This development not only occurs over the short span of the teen years, but it also takes place in front of others, which intensifies a teenager's feelings. Look at the intense feelings that come out of these normal developmental changes.

- ›› Physical changes create embarrassing moments as well as awkwardness, lack of coordination, confusion, and even pain and discomfort as bones, muscles, and organs grow.
- ›› Sexual changes start with rapid, rampant hormonal changes that leave a teenager feeling everything from guilt to amazement.
- ›› Emotional changes create intense emotions—often uncontrollable and uncontrolled.

---

23 Les Parrott, *Helping the Struggling Adolescent* (Grand Rapids, MI: Zondervan Publishing House, 1993) 15-16.

- Social development pushes teenagers to function in an adult world through relationships that alternate from casual to close. Parents are no longer the major focus of a teenager's relationships. Teenagers feel lonely in a crowd and always on display, even when alone.
- Mental growth involves moving from concrete to abstract thinking. Feelings of confusion about what to believe, frustration in not being able to express their thoughts, and excitement in trying on new values dominate this process.
- Spiritual changes include looking for a personal faith that sets a moral standard for a teenager's life. Progressing from doubt to decision can be a long journey of stress, with the teenager often testing different faiths and morals to see how they "fit" who the teenager wants to become.

In addition to the normal developmental process of teenagers, the search for identity is complicated by the diverse ways youth conduct their search. Les Parrott identifies seven of the most common ways in his book *Helping the Struggling Adolescent*. I'm summarizing them here:

- Family Relations—Part of finding out who they are involves pulling away from the family and changing the way they relate to parents and siblings.
- Status Symbols—Possessions not only measure identity, but there is a behavior to accompany each identity. The "party girl" not only has the right clothing and hairstyle, but she does the "party thing."

» Grown-Up Behavior—Teenagers wanting to be adults do adult things, especially previously forbidden activities like smoking, drinking, drugs, and premarital sex.

» Rebellion—Teenagers want to be individuals, different from their parents and even their peers, while maintaining the comfort of the familiar.

» Others' Opinions—The identity the teenager chooses must be validated by others. They often base their identity on how they think others see them.

» Idols—Our celebrity-conscious society offers teenagers a wide variety of stars with whom they can identify.

» Cliquish Exclusion—In an effort to define, overdefine, and redefine themselves, teenagers form relationships that can be intolerant and even cruel.[24]

With all this going on in the lives of teenagers, it's amazing that they have time for relationships. But relationships form the infrastructure of getting along in life.

. . . .

WITH ALL THIS GOING ON IN THE LIVES OF TEENAGERS, IT'S AMAZING THAT THEY HAVE TIME FOR RELATIONSHIPS. BUT RELATIONSHIPS FORM THE INFRASTRUCTURE OF GETTING ALONG IN LIFE.

. . . .

---

24 Parrott, *Helping the Struggling Adolescent*, 16-19.

RELATIONSHIP CONNECTIONS

If needs drive behavior, relationships form the means through which emotional needs are met. The deeper, more intimate the relationship, the greater the possibility that the need will be met, and the teenager will function in a healthy way. Less connected, superficial relationships may result in an unmet need.

• •

IF NEEDS DRIVE BEHAVIOR, RELATIONSHIPS FORM THE MEANS THROUGH WHICH EMOTIONAL NEEDS ARE MET.

• •

Deep, intimate relationships develop most often between a husband and wife, parents and their children, and best friends. To achieve this type of relationship, the people involved must be willing to be open, transparent, and vulnerable. In fact, here's my definition of intimacy—"into-me-you-see." It means allowing another person to get close enough that they see your needs, understand your fears, and know your weaknesses.

A vulnerable relationship means that both people are defenseless before the other because there is a give-and-take in sharing and caring. As one person in the relationship has a need, the other person recognizes and meets that need. Then the process can be reversed. Each time a need is met, the relationship grows closer, deeper, and warmer. We usually think of intimacy as the ultimate relationship in marriage, but that same sense of togetherness or connection happens in relationships with others.

Superficial relationships, on the other hand, happen in situations where there is less opportunity or desire for closeness. These might be the formal relationships established in the business atmosphere, the casual relationships in neighborhoods, or the limited relationships with people whose paths you occasionally cross, such as the teller at your bank or a salesperson in your favorite store. In superficial relationships, neither person expects much, so any needs that are met are usually practical, as opposed to emotional or spiritual. Unfortunately, many families settle for superficial relationships.

Superficial Relationship	Authentic Relationship
indifference	closeness
formal	personal
careful	caring
factually-based	feeling-based
controlled	warm
obscure	transparent
distant	together
nonessential	significant
disposable	lasting
detached	accessible
comfortable	constructive
weak	unique
limited	enthusiastic
satisfactory	inspiring
not always available	connected
sympathetic	empathetic

➻ If you are married, what words describe your relationship with your spouse? (You can use words in the lists or add your own words.)

➻ What words describe your relationship with your teenager?

» What words describe your relationship with a close friend?

» What differences do you notice between the words used to describe your relationships with your spouse, a friend, or your teenager?

RELATIONSHIP TRIANGLES

Sometimes, the complexity of relationships creates problems. What happens when parents disagree about how to relate to their teenager? Maybe one parent is open, warm, and communicative with the teenager about everything, and the other parent prefers to keep information just between the two parents. Or what if parents disagree on how to discipline or when to trust their teenager? They may be participating in what Harriet Lerner, in her book *The Dance of Anger*, calls family triangles that undermine a family's efforts to relate:

In the best of all possible worlds, we envision separate, person-to-person relationships with our friends, coworkers, and family members that were not excessively influenced by other relationships. . . . We would stay out of conflicts between other parties and keep other people from getting in the middle of our own fights. . . . That's the ideal. However, we achieve it only more or less. Triangles are present in all human systems. When anxiety mounts between two people or conflicts begin to surface, a third party will automatically and unconsciously be drawn in. All of us participate in numerous interlocking triangles we are not even aware of. Many of these are not particularly problematic, but one or more may well be.[25]

---

25 Harriet Lerner, Ph.D., *The Dance of Anger: A Woman's Guide to Changing the Patterns of Intimate Relationships* (New York, NY: Harper Perennial, 1997), 162-163.

Here are some triangles parents and teenagers use that can undermine relationships.

» Monte wanted to go to a party after the game. His mom said no, so Monte asked his dad—away from his mother's hearing. Dad didn't ask if Monte had talked with his mother, nor did his dad indicate that he would discuss it with his wife and get back to Monte. Instead, his dad said yes, and Monte was out the door, leaving his parents to fight out who should approve Monte's requests in the future.

» Maryanne was furious with the lack of respect she received at work. When she got home and found no one had made any effort to fix dinner or even to order take-out, she verbally chastised her husband for being thoughtless and her teen daughter for being lazy.

» Bob and Lisa knew they needed to set more structure for their fourteen-year-old son Robert, who showed little desire to make school a priority. Robert lived in front of the computer, playing video games. Bob wanted to put the computer away until Robert brought up his grades. Lisa wanted to monitor his computer time. While they fought over what to do, Robert ignored his homework and played more video games.

» Nick didn't stand a chance when his dad got on his case. Nick's dad called him irresponsible and a disgrace to the family. When Nick's mom heard her husband start in on Nick, she would try to calm her husband down. Then he would verbally attack her. Nick's mother thinks his dad is the problem. ("He fights with Nick all the time.") His dad thinks Nick's mother is the problem. ("She spoils him and won't let him grow up.") Nick thinks he is the problem, and he doesn't know why everyone can't just get along.

The triangle can involve other family members such as siblings, grandparents, and in-laws. The triangle may also involve the teenager, one parent, and an outside source such as the people at school, a boyfriend or girlfriend, or a broken relationship. Triangles pit two of the three players against the other or against one another. Lerner suggests that the problem is the patterns established in these triangular relationships rather than the people. The triangle wouldn't be a problem if there were a deeper desire for connection and flexibility. For example, Nick's mother could stop standing between her husband and her son (unless there is a reason to be concerned about the teenager's physical well-being). Now the father doesn't have an audience to play to, so he may discontinue the nagging. Or Robert's parents could decide to try Lisa's approach for two weeks, and if they see no change in Robert's schoolwork, they could go with Bob's plan.

Sometimes the triangle relationship occurs because of deeper issues between parents. For example, fighting over the teenager's actions may hide the real issue of a parent who is unfaithful, two parents who no longer relate to one another, or a single parent who is overwhelmed with financial concerns. If a triangle pattern has gone on for a long time, however, it may require professional help to sort out the feelings and behaviors.

If you realize that your relationship with your teenager has a poor connection or lacks the warmth, closeness, and understanding of intimate relationships or is part of a triangle, then you may see why it's hard to meet your teenager's needs. On the other hand, a deeper, intimate relationship offers the best way to understand and meet the needs of your teenager. As the adult in the relationship, you take the lead in improving the connection between you and your teenager.

FOUR SKILLS FOR CONNECTED RELATIONSHIPS

Healthy, connected, intimate relationships occur when four skills are developed and used—caring, trusting, giving, and loving. I am basing these relationship skills on the model of four ingredients for marital closeness that I discovered in an excellent guide for developing marital intimacy.[26] As the parent, you can learn to use these skills with your teenager by modeling how they improve relationships. Your teen can then learn to use the same skills in his or her relationships with friends.

1) The Skill of Caring

Caring is about putting yourself in the other person's situation and deciding what will comfort, encourage, and support that person. Empathy is caring's secret weapon. Empathy is a stronger emotion than sympathy. Sympathy says, "I'm sorry that happened to you." Empathy cries with your teenager when they hurt. Empathy takes the deeper step of trying to understand the feelings and thoughts behind the behavior. Empathy does not judge but reflects back the pain it hears.

There are many ways to express caring. Caring involves a personal concern for the other person, so you talk about personal topics. For the teenager, this may be difficult because the teenager is trying to develop

---

26 David and Teresa Ferguson and Chris and Holly Thurman, *Intimate Encounters: A Practical Guide to Discovering the Secrets of a Really Great Marriage* (Nashville, TN: Thomas Nelson Publishers, 1994).

some independence in which Mom and Dad don't know everything they're doing. But the parent can share appropriate personal situations with their teenager, allowing their teenager to also share.

Offering physical, spiritual, and emotional support builds a caring relationship. Tell your teenager you will be praying for him on a day he has a major test. Make an effort to attend the school play your son is in or the debate finals when your daughter participates. Comfort is most often associated with caring. Comfort your teenager by listening; don't feel like you must always have a solution. Affection is the most obvious way to physically express you care. Giving hugs, putting an arm around the shoulder, and even your physical presence can be comforting to a hurting teenager.

Measure your caring skills in your relationship with your teen using the Care Inventory.

	Regularly	Sometimes	A little bit	Never
I praise the accomplishments of my teenager	❏	❏	❏	❏
I comfort my teenager when she is hurting.	❏	❏	❏	❏
I show my affection to my teenager.	❏	❏	❏	❏
I express empathy to my teenager for his sadness, his distress, his pain.	❏	❏	❏	❏
I support my teenager's healthy decisions.	❏	❏	❏	❏

» In my relationship with my teenager, the ways I show I care are _____

_____

» One way I could improve my caring skill is _____

_____

2) The Skill of Trusting

Trust is a major issue between parents and teenagers. Trust measures what's going on in a relationship, like a barometer measures what's going on in the atmosphere. The trust level rises when promises are kept between parents and teenagers. The trust level drops when trust is broken. If a parent regularly fails to keep promises to their teenager, that teenager won't trust their parent. If a teenager breaks curfew, the parents' trust level goes down. In his book *Caring Enough to Confront*, David Augsburger states how vital trust is in a relationship:

> *Trust is the root emotion. In stress, we fall back through the levels of fidelity, competence, adequacy, courage, initiative, autonomy, will, hope until we encounter the fundamental ground of our being: trust.*
>
> *"I trust you." When I hear—or sense—that message from another person I feel loved, I feel accepted, I feel respected.*
>
> *"I don't trust you." When I receive that message from someone important to me, I feel disliked, cut off, rejected.*[27]

The keyword for the trusting skill is openness. Trust grows from constant communication of what is expected—then seeing the other person live up to those expectations. Two of the major enemies of trust are false assumptions and rejection. If a teenager

---

27 David Augsburger, *Caring Enough to Confront* (Ventura, CA: Regal Books, 1983), 64.

stays out past curfew, assuming that Mom and Dad will understand, he is in danger of breaking trust. If a parent doesn't keep a commitment to do something with the teenager, the teenager feels rejected.

Trusting is a two-way street. Not only do you need to trust your teenager, but your teenager needs to trust you. You prove yourself trustworthy as a parent when you are honest with your family, by following through on commitments, by resolving conflict in a healthy manner, by keeping your marriage vows, by not judging until you've heard both sides of the story, and so on. Your consistent daily living tells your teenager you are trustworthy. Your teenager becomes trustworthy by completing the tasks assigned to her, by living within the guidelines and expectations agreed to by the two of you, and by being honest with you, just to name a few.

Teenagers often complain, "You don't trust me!" And that may be true, particularly if the teenager has a history of being untrustworthy. You can face this issue of trusting your teenager by making two lists. On one, write the areas where you feel you can trust the teenager. On the second, write areas or actions where you have not seen growth. Share the lists with your teenager. Say something like, "Here's where I see maturity and am willing to trust you. Here are areas you need to work on for me to trust you further." As trust is earned, trust should be given.

• •

AS TRUST IS EARNED, TRUST SHOULD BE GIVEN.

• •

When trust is broken, your reaction is critical. Do you blow up or simmer? Do you punish immediately or step back and get a broader picture? Was a false assumption made? What information from you will straighten out that false assumption? Was rejection involved? Was the teenager rejecting you by his actions? Was the teenager feeling rejected? Once a trust is broken, it takes time to restore. Assigning small tasks and seeing results earns trust. As trust grows, encourage your teenager by saying things that express your growing level of trust:

» "I appreciate your following through with your commitment to babysit tonight, even though your friends had last-minute plans."
» "You're doing your homework faithfully, and it has improved your grades."

Talk with the teenager about setting personal boundaries in life. Discuss the boundaries or limitations you place on your life. State how you can be trusted to set boundaries for the teenager at this time, turning over areas to the teenager who demonstrates trustworthy actions by living within the boundaries.

Sometimes when the teenager says, "You don't trust me!" our response is, "I trust you; I don't trust other people." Ross Campbell explains how to help your teenager understand your response:

First, allow privileges based upon the trust relationship. Secondly, try to make sure your teenager can handle the particular situation, before you allow him to go. . . . Checking into the appropriateness of the situation does not mean you do not trust your teenager. Even though a teenager is trustworthy, means well, and has fine

intentions, there are still situations he may not have the maturity to
handle. In these cases, you must protect your teenager.[28]

When Sherry and Linda wanted to spend the week at the beach with their friends for spring break, their mother wouldn't let her fifteen- and seventeen-year-olds go. "I trust you to act like the girls I know you are and whom I have raised. But I know what happens during spring breaks at the beach. Others throw away their morals and get caught up in activities and behaviors that are dangerous and morally wrong. Because I love you, I can't let you go to the beach during spring break, but let's find something else to do that you will enjoy."

Measure your trusting skills in your relationship with your teenager by completing the trust inventory.

	Regularly	Sometimes	A little bit	Never
I trust my teenager to make smart, healthy decisions.	❏	❏	❏	❏
My teenager trusts me to keep his personal secrets.	❏	❏	❏	❏
I can be trusted to follow through on my commitments to my teenager.	❏	❏	❏	❏
I act in the best interest of my teenager.	❏	❏	❏	❏
I share the time and ways I trust God with my teenager.	❏	❏	❏	❏

28 Ross Campbell, *How to Really Love Your Teenager* (Wheaton, IL: Victor Books, 1981), 80-81.

›› In my relationship with my teenager, the ways I show trust are _____

_____

›› One way I could improve my trusting skill is _____

_____

3) The Skill of Giving

Connected relationships depend on giving. In most relationships, your meeting another's needs results in that person responding by meeting your needs. Teenagers are a different story. Because they struggle to handle their emotions, deal with the rapid changes in their lives, and get their own needs met, teenagers will neither be able to recognize nor meet your needs, and you should not expect them to.

As the parent, you are the primary one to keep your teenager's emotional tank filled in ways we've already talked about. Don't deny, however, that you have your own needs. This is why a strong, healthy, life-giving marriage relationship is so important. If you're single, you can also turn to close friends, other family members, or even your church family to refill your emotional and relational tank. Ultimately, looking to God and leaning on Him is the greatest source for satisfying our every need.

Giving to your teenager can benefit you in several unique ways. For example, you might experience feelings of comfort when you are able to help your teen. You can feel encouraged when you see change in your teenager because of your efforts to meet an important need you know they have in their life. You can find hope in watching your teenager grow more secure and confident as needs are met in a healthy way. You can feel grateful for the qualities you appreciate in your teenager. Later, within the strong, connected relationship between an adult parent and an adult child, you may even experience times when your adult child recognizes and meets your needs, but that time is for the future. Presently, you give, and your teenager receives.

• •

BECAUSE THEY STRUGGLE TO HANDLE THEIR EMOTIONS, DEAL WITH THE RAPID CHANGES IN THEIR LIVES, AND GET THEIR OWN NEEDS MET, TEENAGERS WILL NEITHER BE ABLE TO RECOGNIZE NOR MEET YOUR NEEDS, AND YOU SHOULD NOT EXPECT THEM TO.

• •

As you develop the skill of giving, look for ways to build a relationship between the two of you and the family. Surprise your teenager by doing the unexpected. For example, provide a high-energy snack for a late night of studying, fill your teenager's car with gas, or leave a gift card on her pillow for a movie and a meal of her choice. Give by expressing appreciation for your teenager often and openly as well as to the family and others. As part of the skill of giving, involve your teenager in activities that allow him to give to others, such as feeding the homeless or volunteering at a children's hospital.

Measure your giving skills in your relationship with your teenager by completing the giving inventory:

	Regularly	Sometimes	A little bit	Never
I give focused attention to my teenager on a daily basis.	❏	❏	❏	❏
I recognize times of stress in my teenager's life and give encouragement.	❏	❏	❏	❏
I include my teenager in times of volunteer service or ministry to others.	❏	❏	❏	❏
I express appreciation to my teenager for a job well done.	❏	❏	❏	❏
I openly express thanks for all God has given me and my family.	❏	❏	❏	❏

» In my relationship with my teenager, the ways I give are ____

_____

_____

» One way I could improve my giving skill is _____

_____

4) The Skill of Loving

The final skill includes all aspects of love: affection, touch, attention, availability, caring, and appreciation. There are so many ways to share love with your teenager. An important aspect of loving is to understand what kind of love your teenager wants and will respond to. Dr. Gary Chapman has written a book—*The Five Love Languages of Teenagers*—that explains five languages "spoken" by parents. According to Chapman, your teenager will respond to one of these languages more frequently than to the others. When your teenager's preferred language of love is spoken, your teenager will feel loved. Let me summarize these languages briefly. Perhaps you will recognize your teenager's love language response.

Love Language 1—"Physical Touch" is naturally given most often to small children in hugs and kisses and tender touches. When children become teenagers, however, the physical touches may not be as important as the other four languages. Brief touches as you pass by a teenager's chair during their homework, a back massage or back-scratching, or combing a teenager's hair are all physical ways to express love to your teenager who might reject hugs and kisses. Some teenagers, however, enjoy physical affection and hugging; this language is their primary way of feeling loved.

Love Language 2—"Words of Affirmation" encourage and affirm your teenager to keep going when times get tough and to hang in there when they feel like quitting. Teenagers who need this language are those who want verbal assurance of their parent's love and support.

Love Language 3—"Quality Time" gives your teenager undivided attention for a period of time. Teenagers recognize this language when they feel their parent is available and willing to listen when their teenager wants to talk. The security of knowing their parent is available helps this teenager feel loved.

Love Language 4—"Giving and Receiving Gifts" is often spoken by busy parents who find it easier to buy and give gifts than to get involved in the lives of their teenagers. These parents might be surprised to find that some teenagers would rather have quality time or words of affirmation. However, there are teenagers who understand the love behind the gift and see the gift as an expression of love.

Love Language 5—"Acts of Service" expresses love through actions that show help and support to their teenager. Parents share this kind of love when they work on their teenager's car together, bake their teenager's favorite cake, or help with a science project, for example. A teenager who recognizes these acts of service feels loved and supported.[29]

As you can see, love can be expressed in many ways. When the home environment is built on unconditional love, a teenager can find a healthy filling station for their emotional tank, and their emotional gauges operate properly in a neutral position rather than on red alert.

Measure your loving skills in your relationship with your teenager by completing the loving inventory:

	Regularly	Sometimes	A little bit	Never
I show open, but appropriate, affection to my teenager.	❏	❏	❏	❏
I try to make eye contact with my teenager.	❏	❏	❏	❏
I tell my teenager of my love for him/her.	❏	❏	❏	❏
I willingly do an activity to show my teenager my love.	❏	❏	❏	❏
I give my teenager unconditional love.	❏	❏	❏	❏

---

29 Gary Chapman, "Teen Love Languages," *Living with Teenagers*, February 1998, 11-12.

» In my relationship with my teenager, the ways I show love are _____

_____

» One way I could improve my loving skill is _____

_____

RELATIONSHIP BLUNDERS

Parents sometimes make it difficult for teens to develop a close relationship. These parents often think they are helping, but they actually harm their relationship in ways they may not even realize.

The Rescuer

This parent damages the parent-teen relationship by not letting their teenager grow up. In an effort to protect, this parent prevents their teenager from experiencing the natural consequences of poor decisions. Dad frequently gives his daughter an extra $20 when her allowance doesn't last through the week. Mom constantly yells at her teenager to get up in the morning, so he won't miss the school bus. Dad works on a science project late into the night because his teenager procrastinated.

Rescuers who continually bail out their teenagers feel angry at their teenager for being irresponsible. Underneath, however, rescuers usually fear that their teenagers won't need them or depend on them anymore. Les Christie reminds us:

[Teenagers] should be equipped with the personal strength needed to see the demands imposed on them by their school, peer group, part-time job and later in other adult responsibilities.

Our goal as parents is for our kids to be truly responsible for their own behavior.[30]

The Passive Parent

The opposite type of parent from the rescuer is the parent who does nothing. This parent stopped parenting their teenager for a variety of reasons, some of which may include involvement in a personal crisis such as divorce, job loss, taking care of an elderly parent, being unaware of how to parent a teenager, or feeling overwhelmed by tough parenting problems. It is also possible for the passive parent to live with a more aggressive spouse who takes over the parenting responsibilities. This can set up the destructive triangle relationship discussed earlier. Although teenagers say they want freedom from their parents, they don't want parents to check out altogether. Teenagers view a lack of involvement as a lack of care.

The Mixed Messenger

This parent damages their parent-teen relationship by sending mixed messages. I know parents who criticize their teenagers for looking at their phones nonstop but are guilty of texting while driving or scrolling through their emails or social media while eating dinner at home or at a restaurant. What the parent says (their disapproval) and what the parent allows represent opposing messages. Families are not the only ones guilty of sending mixed messages.

The media sends mixed messages. (A commercial for sexual abstinence among teenagers runs during a TV show whose

---

30 Les Christie, "Positive Discipline," *Living with Teenagers*, July 1998, 14.

characters end up in bed after the first date.) The schools send mixed messages. (Grades matter most, but if you don't ace the standardized test, SAT, or ACT, kiss your chances goodbye for getting in your college of choice.) Even the church can send mixed messages. (Bring your friends, but be sure they look like us and talk like us.) Mixed-messenger parents wonder why they can't get their teenagers to stick with commitments.

The Popular Parent

This parent damages the parent-teen relationship by wanting to be liked by their teenager. They equate parenting responsibilities with negative feelings and "being friends" with their teenager with positive feelings. Mom wants a best friend. Dad wants a golfing buddy. But teenagers don't necessarily want parents who dress, talk, or act like they do. God established the order of the parent-child relationship. (See Ephesians 6:1-4.) The child learns from the parent. These parents may think their relationships with their teenagers are healthy—until they try to discipline their teenagers, and the relationships rip apart. Don't misunderstand. Parents and teenagers should be able to share, connect, have fun, and laugh and cry together, but you are the adult, the parent, and the one providing leadership, boundaries, guidance, and love.

The Pitiful Parent

This parent is a variation of the popular parent. As the child grows to look more like an adult, this parent expects an adult relationship. This lonely parent may have trouble relating to other adults, so the parent depends on the teenager for companionship.

Burdened by problems unrelated to the teenager, this parent may expect their teenager to become the parent's priest, hearing confessions of confusion or inappropriate actions or even seeking advice. Tending to be lenient, this parent takes the position of "How could you do this to me?" when the teenager does something that requires discipline. I sometimes see this in single-parent homes where the parents live with unusually heavy schedules and little time to develop adult friendships, so they turn to the more convenient teenager at home.

The Dictator

This parent desires ultimate control. Rules form the focal point of control. This parent tries to dictate and control their teenager's every decision. This parent destroys communication with dictums and creates rebellion instead of a relationship. Dictators don't let their teenager participate in making the rules or in making personal decisions. Les Christie states how this parent ought to look at boundaries and rules:

Fair and reasonable discipline is like a fence providing and defining limits and demonstrates care and concern. . . . The fence should not be so close to the house that it stifles creativity, yet not so far away that teens can do virtually anything they want.[31]

There are other parenting blunders that cut communication lines:

>> The embarrassing parent whose behavior, attitude, or addiction is painfully embarrassing to the teenager.
>> The "favoritist" who openly displays a preference for one child over the other.

---

31 Christie, "Positive Discipline," 16.

▸▸ The explosive parent whose anger can never be understood, anticipated, or controlled.

▸▸ The critical parent who speaks only in words of criticism.

These are the types of parents youth do not want.

In contrast, Walt Mueller, in *Understanding Today's Youth Culture*, offers a list of what teens actually do want from their parents. Teenagers want:

▸▸ Parents who don't argue in front of them.

▸▸ Parents who treat each family member the same.

▸▸ Parents who are honest.

▸▸ Parents who are tolerant of others.

▸▸ Parents who welcome their friends to the home.

▸▸ Parents who build a team spirit with their children.

▸▸ Parents who answer their questions.

▸▸ Parents who give punishment when needed but not in front of others—especially their friends.

▸▸ Parents who concentrate on good points instead of weaknesses.

▸▸ Parents who are consistent.[32]

RELATIONSHIP BUILDING

I hope you've seen how a vital, dynamic relationship provides the atmosphere for meeting needs. When God created people with needs, He also knew that one person could not be totally responsible for meeting another person's needs. God's plan to take care of that huge responsibility begins with the family, but as Christians,

---

32 Walt Mueller, *Understanding Today's Youth Culture* (Wheaton, IL: Tyndale House, 1994), 340.

you can also depend on God's family, the church. Fellow believers working through the various ministries of the local church offer healthy sources for getting your teenager's needs met.

In addition to letting your local church family help you in your parenting journey, you can work at building healthy parenting skills, but it takes time and effort. Walt Mueller suggests that parents continually ask the question, "How can I begin to break through the walls?"[33] It takes knowing your teenager's world, understanding their development, and cutting through the confusion. Here is a checklist to see how you're doing at breaking through the walls and building relationships.

Learn How the Secular World Impacts Your Teenager

» Do you visit your teenager's school for meetings and workshops or to volunteer to help serve on the school campus?

» Do you know what music, YouTube videos, or video games your teenagers are listening to, watching, or participating in?

» What messages is social media delivering to your teenager?

» What temptations and risks confront your teenager regularly?

Look at Experiences From the Teenager's Point of View

» What personal stress or anxiety does your teenager feel? Where does that stress come from?

» Is your teenager worried about an ailing grandparent or an unemployed parent?

» Are keeping up with grades and too many activities causing stress, depression, lack of sleep, or strained relationships?

---

33 Walt Mueller, *Understanding Today's Youth Culture*, 340.

» Is a job placing extra pressure on your teenager?

» Have you met your teenager's friends? What are their concerns, stresses, and problems?

Gain an Unbiased Perspective on Your Teenager

» Ask other adults who are around your teen to assess your teenager's needs.

» Are you surprised by what you hear?

» Are you willing to listen for the grain of truth without defending past mistakes?

» How can you use this broader perspective to establish a strong relationship with your teenager?

Keep in Mind the Rapid Changes in Your Teenager's Development

Unfortunately, numerical years don't indicate emotional maturity. You never know if you're talking to a fourteen-year-old acting like a ten-year-old today who will act like an eighteen-year-old tomorrow. They are in the process of becoming adults; they haven't arrived yet.

» How do the rapid changes in your teenager's development influence his or her needs?

» How can you help your teenager understand these changes?

» How are you staying informed of what developmental stage your teenager may be experiencing?

Don't wait for their emotional tanks to get too low. Keep refilling through positive strokes.

• •

DON'T WAIT FOR THEIR EMOTIONAL TANKS TO GET TOO LOW. KEEP REFILLING THROUGH POSITIVE STROKES.

• •

It's been said that it takes eight compliments to make up for the emotional damage done by one critical remark. Christie reminds us:

Look for progress, not simply the finished product. Teens get excited when they know you see them progressing in some good direction. . . . Don't reward teens for good behavior with food or overly gushy insincere praise. They need to do good because good is good to do. They don't need rewards; they need encouragement. They need feedback. It comes in three forms: compliments, comments, and constructive criticism. You may say, "This is wrong, but I know you can fix it."[34]

Teach teens—especially daughters—to express their needs. This skill can be accomplished by using two questions:

1) "On a scale from zero to ten (ten being the best), where would you rate our relationship today?" Asking your teen this question provides a picture of the current state of the relationship.

2) "What are some specific things Mom or Dad could do over the next week that would move us closer to a ten?" This question is the crucial one.[35]

---

34 Christie, "Positive Discipline," 16.
35 Gary and Greg Smalley, "The Secret to Raising Teenagers: A Bountiful Bank Account!" *Living with Teenagers*, July 1998, 26.

As you come to the close of this section on understanding your teenager, pause to reflect on the challenging words of 1 John 3:18: "Dear children, let us not love with words or tongue but with actions and in truth." Then spend time completing this section.

» An action I need to take to strengthen my relationship with my teenager is _____

_____

» A truth about my teenager that I now see clearly is _____

_____

_____

» Start the relationship-building process by reflecting on the things that you appreciate or admire about your teenager. Write a brief note of appreciation to your teen stating these qualities for which you are thankful and give it to them.

» Based on what you've learned so far, make a "Hopeful List" of what you'd like to see happen with your teenager.

_____

_____

_____

_____

_____

_____

_____

_____

_____

MOVING ON

At this point, I hope you've gained several insights into what's happening in your teenager's life beyond their surface behavior. At the same time, you may be wondering about your own needs—met and unmet—and how these influence your ability to parent. A vital step in meeting the needs of your teenager involves understanding your unmet needs, both in the past and at present. Before sharing specific ideas for meeting the needs of your teenager, you must understand how your own unmet needs color your relationships, attitudes, and actions. The next part, "Understanding Yourself," provides a way to work through these tough but highly significant issues.

PART 2

UNDERSTANDING YOURSELF

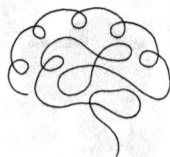

CHAPTER 6
LOOKING IN
THE MIRROR

John looked on with great sadness as other parents greeted their teenagers returning from a week at camp with welcoming hugs and kisses. John's dad walked up behind John and abruptly asked, "Where's your gear?" No hug. No, "Glad you're home." Just, "Where's your gear?" The commotion of getting everything together and saying goodbyes and thank-yous swept the sadness from John's mind momentarily.

Later, when he was alone, he thought again about how his dad never hugged him or told him he loved him. With one year left before he leaves for college, John feels a desperate need to share his feelings with his dad. John realizes that in his efforts to get his parents' attention, he has hurt his family with several defiant actions. Deep down, however, he longs to be hugged by his dad. He can't understand why his dad won't show him any affection.

I know John's dad. His strict home environment allows for limited physical contact and very little verbalized affection. His dad believes in hard work, helping others, and keeping to himself.

John's dad wasn't born knowing how to parent. He learned his parenting skills from John's grandfather. Parenting is a learned behavior based on what you see modeled at home. Unless you make a deliberate effort to understand your past and change your reactions, you will repeat the behavior modeled by your parents. If you had healthy parenting role models, you learned healthy parenting practices. But none of us had perfect parents, so along the way, we learned imperfect parenting behavior.

Extreme cases of poor parenting occur when the parent's parenting is either abusive (physically, emotionally, sexually, or mentally) or based on an addiction to alcohol, drugs, pornography, gambling, or some other destructive situation. Unfortunately, we now know that children raised in an abusive or addictive environment have a tendency to repeat the abusive, addictive behavior—even though, as children, they were hurt by their parent's behavior.

WHEN I GROW UP AND BECOME A PARENT, I'LL NEVER . . .

How did you complete that sentence when you were a teenager? Are you parenting the way you said you'd NEVER parent?

» Do you wonder why you end up yelling at your teenager?
» Are you uncomfortable about encouraging your teenager?
» Do you relate to your teenager through teasing, even though she's asked you to stop?

➤ Are you struggling with finding good things to like about your teenager?

➤ Are you compelled to give your teenager advice during every discussion?

➤ Why is it hard for you to comfort your teenager when he is hurting?

➤ Do you lecture your teenager repeatedly on the same topic (also called nagging)?

Are you looking in the mirror and seeing your parent? Don't give up! There's hope for recovery, change, and growth. The next three chapters are vital to meeting your teenager's needs. If you skip these chapters or avoid completing the activities, you will find it difficult to meet your teenager's needs effectively.

• •

WHETHER WE LIKE IT OR NOT, WE ARE PRODUCTS OF OUR PAST. UNDERSTANDING THAT PAST MAKES THE FUTURE BRIGHTER.

• •

Whether we like it or not, we are products of our past. Understanding that past makes the future brighter.

Look in the Mirror and Discover

➤ *You cannot give what you do not have.* If your parents failed to comfort you over broken relationships or teenage disappointments or during times of intense stress, you will have a hard time recognizing your teenager's need for comfort.

Have you tried to comfort your teenager, but it felt so awkward that you gave up?

» *You are responsible for the emotional environment in your home.* Your ability to parent effectively depends on your creating an emotionally healthy environment. If the environment where you grew up met your needs, then you're more likely to recognize and meet your teenager's needs effectively. If, however, your emotional childhood environment was unhealthy, and your needs were not met at home, you may not know how to recognize and meet your teenager's needs. If your parents didn't respect your privacy, listened in on your phone calls, and demanded your presence at family events, it may be hard for you to give your teenager the space and privacy needed for them to feel respected in your home.

» *You can change.* You can look at the past, take the ideas and actions that worked, throw away the stuff that didn't work, and learn new parenting skills. You can learn how to provide a home environment that is healthy and meets your teenager's needs.

» *You can develop a more open, honest relationship with your teenager.* By looking at your past and dealing with its pain, you will be able to recognize your teenager's struggles more often. Knowing what not to do is just as important as knowing what you can do.

» *Your present-day relationship with your parents can develop into a true adult relationship.* You will no longer feel like a hurting child. You may even realize how to meet the emotional needs of your parents as they grow older.

➤ *You will see how to get your needs met in healthy ways.* As a result, you will be able to relate to others, recognize their needs, and possibly meet those needs in return.

➤ *You will develop an appreciation for the positive qualities in your family* as you identify their strengths and acknowledge their care.

➤ *You can realize that you are an imperfect person raised in an imperfect environment by imperfect people, but you survived.*[36] As a result, you will never be a perfect parent (maybe a pretty terrific parent or a better-than-average parent, but never perfect!)

Be Honest About Your Past

When remembering their pasts, most people either idealize these events or push the bad experiences away, refusing to remember them. Does the word *hurt* immediately stir up painful memories of your childhood and teenage years? I challenge you to look beneath the surface reflection in your mirror and be honest about your real past. In this chapter, you will be evaluating relationships with your parents and others. Identifying the pain in these relationships does not blame anyone. You are dealing with facts. This experience is not about blame; it's about healing.

Everyone experiences emotional pain. Instead of asking the question, "Have you been hurt in the past?" I'll be focusing on, "Have you identified the hurt and looked for ways to find healing?" To answer this last question, you will need objectivity—reality, not perception. How can you gain objectivity, especially if you've been running from your past? One way is to let others help you. Ask a brother or sister what they remember about your parents

---

36 David Ferguson, *Parenting with Intimacy Workbook* (Wheaton, IL: Victor Books, 1995).

or about certain events. Ask other family members who often saw you and your parents together. If you are still in the church where you grew up, maybe other people in your church can give insight. Don't stay in denial. Be honest, and accept the healing.

"When I Was a Teenager . . . ,"

First, look at your teenage years. Although many of your needs could have gone unmet in your childhood, your teenage years gave your parents a second chance to meet your needs. When needs continued to go unmet, you reacted through your behavior. In the space below, list the actions you did as a teenager that were unproductive, inappropriate, or high-risk. For example, you may list smoking, running with a crowd with different standards than yours, lying to parents, driving too fast, or having sex before marriage. This is *your* list. No one else will see it, so be as honest as you can. You may have more or fewer than ten actions.

1) _____

2) _____

3) _____

4) _____

5) _____

6) _____

7) _____

8) _____

9) _____

10) _____

Beside each behavior, write down an unmet need you feel was linked to that behavior. For example, beside *smoking*, you may list the need *to feel like an adult*. Using the thinking, feeling, and behaving pattern I discussed in chapter 3. Reflect on negative behaviors you listed above, and complete these sentences.

» I remember a time when I most needed my mom to _____
_____ and she didn't.
» That made me think that my mom _____.
» That made me feel _____ about my mom.
» As a result, I behaved _____.
» The way my mom related to my behavior as a teenager was to
_____.
» I wish she had _____.
» Have you ever discussed this with your mom? _____
» If so, what was the result? _____

Respond to the same questions focusing on your father.

» I remember a time when I most needed my dad to _____
_____ and he didn't.
» That made me think that my dad _____.
» That made me feel _____ about my dad.
» As a result, I behaved _____.
» The way my dad related to my behavior as a teenager was to
_____.
» I wished he had _____.
» Have you ever discussed this with your dad? _____
» If so, what was the result? _____

The Needs of My Teenage Years

Let's evaluate how your needs were met during your teenage years. Remember: you are not accusing or blaming; you are seeking healing. Healing begins when the hurt is faced. In some cases, perhaps one parent met your needs, but the other one didn't. In other cases, you may feel that neither parent met your needs. Others in the family or outside of the family could have satisfied your needs.

• •

HEALING BEGINS WHEN THE HURT IS FACED.

• •

In the chart below, check the box by the person or category that expresses who met each need. Don't hurry this evaluation; it's not a timed event. You may want to look through old photos as you think about your teenage years.

Who met this need in your life	Mom	Dad	Someone Else	No One
Attention	❏	❏	❏	❏
Respect	❏	❏	❏	❏
Valued	❏	❏	❏	❏
Appreciation	❏	❏	❏	❏
Nurtured	❏	❏	❏	❏
Supported	❏	❏	❏	❏
Comfort	❏	❏	❏	❏

Who met this need in your life	Mom	Dad	Someone Else	No One
Significance and purpose	❏	❏	❏	❏
Security	❏	❏	❏	❏
Acceptance	❏	❏	❏	❏
Loved	❏	❏	❏	❏

➤ What was your greatest need growing up?

➤ Who met that need most of the time for you?

➤ How did you feel about your unmet needs as a teenager?

➤ From an adult perspective, how do you feel about those unmet needs today?

➤ Most of the time, I felt that my mom _____ me.

➤ Most of the time, I felt that my dad _____ me.

The Needs of My Adult Years

Just as I've been sharing how needs drive your teenager's behavior, you can see firsthand how your needs motivated your behavior as a teenager. The same is true for adult behavior. Most adults usually behave in acceptable ways. But when you don't get anywhere with your first behavior, you may show your real needs through your reactions. Have you ever wondered: *Why did I fly off the handle like that? Why did his answer make me so angry? Where did that thought (or action) come from? I didn't mean to do that!* Behind these surprise actions and reactions are your unmet needs.

Write down the primary emotional need you feel is missing in your life today. It might be something like one of these.

I need:

» To feel appreciated for all I do _____.

» To be respected by my children _____.

» To feel secure in my marriage _____.

» To know someone cares about me. To be accepted even though I'm not perfect _____.

» To feel I can share my hurt with someone who understands.

My primary emotional need is _____
_____.

This primary need influences your life more than you realize. Bobb Biehl, in his book *Why You Do What You Do*, identifies several areas in our lives affected by the desire to get this primary need met.

1) Your primary need influences your decisions. You select one choice over another because you think it will help you get your primary need met. Or you may realize that your choice will push you away from your main need. For example, you might make a career decision by asking questions like this: "Will this new job make me feel significant?" "Will others accept me as a leader now?" "Will I receive the respect I desire?"

2) Your primary need influences your ability to listen. You selectively hear what you want to based on your primary needs. If your primary need is acceptance, you may hear "I like you as a person" when someone merely compliments your clothing.

3) Your primary need influences the way you judge relationships. Getting your primary need met especially colors the person you choose as a marriage partner. It also plays into your friendships with those who can meet your primary need.

4) Your primary need influences which group you join. You will look for a group where you feel comfortable and accepted. The group instinctively feels like "my kind of people."

5) Your primary need influences how you handle your life. Getting your primary need met will drive the decision to continue the way you are or to change. If you decide you cannot go on without getting that need met, that change is often called "a midlife crisis."

6) Your primary need influences why you feel emotionally "driven." For example, if your primary gauge is for recognition, you may become a workaholic, determined to earn your superior's recognition at the cost of time with the family.

7) Your primary need influences the way you handle incredible adversity or disappointment. When you believe your actions, decisions, or efforts will help you meet a goal that fulfills your emotional need, and it doesn't, how do you feel? Devastated? Disappointed? For example, you may buy a car hoping to feel accepted and significant. But that feeling will be fleeting. Or you may work hard to earn a top goal in sales, hoping to feel important, but after all the celebration, there is a let-down.[37]

Now, let's look at all your present needs using the same gauges you used in evaluating your teenager's needs. Below are the five basic gauges and the related needs. Beside each need, write a number from one to ten that indicates how well you feel this need is being met in your life. A "1" indicates the need is not being met; a "10" indicates the need is being met. Take your time as you think through these needs.

---

37 Bobb Biehl, *Why You Do What You Do* (Nashville, TN: Thomas Nelson Publishers, 1993) 68-72

1) The Noticed Gauge

_____ I need focused attention that indicates

_____ I am respected as a person, valued for who I am, and appreciated for what I do.

2) The Encouragement Gauge

_____ I need to be nurtured as I reach for my dreams and supported when I feel like giving up.

3) The Empathy Gauge

_____ I need to receive comfort when I experience pain, sorrow, or despair.

4) The Direction Gauge

_____ I need to feel a sense of significance and purpose in my life

5) The Security Gauge

_____ I need to feel physical security as well as acceptance, regardless of my flaws and mistakes, and loved no matter what

Perhaps these gauges don't cover a specific need you have. Great! That means you're thinking. Write the need you feel is missing in your life and a rating here:

» The need is _____.

» I rate it _____.

Based on the numbers you chose for each need, circle your top three needs. (These will be the needs having the lowest numbers beside them). From these three needs, select your primary need. This is the one need that deserves immediate attention. Write that need here:

» My primary emotional need is _____.
» Who do you think can meet this emotional need in your life today? _____

WHAT'S COMING UP

In chapter 7, you will see how to heal the hurt you've identified by evaluating your needs. In chapter 8, you will find ways to get those present-day unmet needs satisfied and how this prepares you to meet the needs of your teenagers.

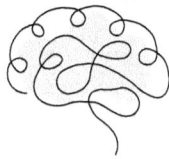

LOOKING AT THE PAST

When you were growing up, what was your fantasy about your future? Did you picture yourself living in the perfect family, with a nice house, a great job, a luxury brand car in your driveway, a loving, devoted spouse, and perfect children? Or did a "happily ever after" fantasy never even cross your mind? Most of us fall somewhere between perfect fantasies and no fantasy at all when it comes to what we expected out of life. Are the fantasies of your childhood and teenage years coming true?

FACING REALITY

Facing your past can be a scary, difficult, and painful experience. When you think back to your teenage years, do you remember the fun, the good times, and the great interaction with your folks? Have you reconstructed a fantasy world of your teenage years?

Possibly. Or was your past so difficult and dark that you prefer to ignore it? Are you willing to look beyond your past fantasies (good or bad) in order to find healing and closure? Which statement best describes your feelings about the past?

"Why look back? I can't change my parents, and I can't change the past."

"But I can do something about the future."

• •

YOU WILL NOT BE ABLE TO CHANGE PAST EVENTS, BUT YOU CAN EVALUATE THE PAST, FIND HEALING FROM THE HURTS OF THE PAST, ACKNOWLEDGE HOPE IN THE POSITIVE MEMORIES, AND WORK TOWARD MAKING YOUR FUTURE BETTER.

• •

That last statement is one to build on. You will not be able to change past events, but you can evaluate the past, find healing from the hurts of the past, acknowledge hope in the positive memories, and work toward making your future better. Before looking at specific issues related to your parents, reflect on several events in your teenage years.

>> What was your greatest achievement during your teenage years?

>> What was your most difficult experience?

>> What was your biggest disappointment as a teenager?

» What person, event, or situation made you angry most often?

» What person, event, or situation helped you laugh most often?

» What is your favorite (or most painful) memory of being thirteen years old?

» What is your favorite (or most painful) memory of being sixteen years old?

» What is your favorite (or most painful) memory of being eighteen years old?

» Who was the most influential person in your teenage years?

Looking at the past may stir up feelings you've tried to avoid or thought you'd handled long ago. You may feel angry, frustrated, discouraged, or cursed—a wide range of negative emotions. Don't let the past pull you down. Your job is to face the past, so you can look toward the future. You began reading this book with the idea of learning how to help your teenager. As you understand your past, you become more sensitive and aware of your teenager's present and future. By learning what needs went unmet and unresolved in your life, you can recognize what needs are going unmet in your teenager's life.

For example, if you felt unappreciated as a teenager, you will not recognize your teenager's need to feel appreciated unless you have faced the reality of your own lack of appreciation. Beware of the other extreme, however. Once you realize what needs went unmet in your life, don't overcompensate by flooding attention on your unsuspecting teenager. Keep a healthy balance of all the emotional gauges.

Looking at your past helps you accept the fact that you are not the perfect parent. (You may have thought about this already but hesitated to accept the idea.) Congratulations! Not being perfect means you still need God; it means you still need others.

Looking at the past may change your relationship with your parents. Instead of keeping your parents in a fantasy position on those parental pedestals, you can let your parents jump down and become real people in your life. You can relate to your parents one adult to another, rather than as a child to a parent.

YOUR FAMILY MEMORIES

In the previous chapter, I explained that your ability to parent is based on the skills you learned from others, particularly your parents. A *USA Today* poll indicates where we've learned our parenting skills:

- » Our Parents—45%
- » Relatives, Friends, and Spouses—35%
- » Books and Magazines—34%
- » Religious Faith—24%
- » Bible—11%
- » Other—13%
- » Not Sure—6%[38]

---

38 "Where Are Parenting Skills Learned?" from USA *Today*, 05/02/98, as quoted in *Youthworker*, May/June 1998, 18.

• •

YOUR HOME ENVIRONMENT WHEN YOU WERE A CHILD STRONGLY INFLUENCES THE ENVIRONMENT IN YOUR HOME TODAY.

• •

Your home environment when you were a child strongly influences the environment in your home today. Your feelings about your home when you were a teenager may be both positive and negative. Perhaps you felt more comfortable with your mother than your father or vice versa. Or you may have had only one parent to relate to, at times feeling comfortable with that parent, at other times, feeling uncomfortable.

» When you were fifteen, who made you feel most comfortable? _____
   Why? _____
» When you were seventeen, who made you feel most comfortable? _____
   Why? _____
» When you were nineteen, who made you feel most comfortable? _____
   Why? _____

You've already seen how your thoughts, feelings, and behaviors as a teenager grew out of unmet needs, especially when your emotional tank was empty. Evaluate your thoughts and feelings about your parents and your behaviors toward them at specific times in your teenage years.

» What is your favorite memory of your dad?

» Why is this event a favorite?

» How did you feel about your dad at the time of this event?

» How did you act toward your dad at the time of this event?

» What made you most angry at your dad?

» What made you most frightened about your dad?

» When were you most happy around your dad?

» Did you know that your dad loved you? How?

» What is your favorite memory of your mom?

» Why is this event a favorite?

» How did you feel about your mom at the time of this event?

» How did you act toward your mom at the time of this event?

» What made you most angry at your mom?

» What made you most frightened about your mom?

» When were you most happy around your mom?

» Did you know that your mom loved you? How?

» Which parent took the lead in parenting you during your teen years?

» Has any event in your teenage past kept you from a healthy relationship with your parents today?

From the adult perspective of today, what do you think about these events, thoughts, feelings, and behaviors? Were your feelings accurate? Were your actions appropriate?

CAUGHT IN THE PARENT TRAP

Probably one of the biggest fantasies in your later teenage years was that someone would come along and marry you and take over all your neglected needs. For example, if you felt rejected by your parents, you probably married someone who accepted you the way you were. In your marriage, however, you already know that when your spouse disagrees with you or rejects an idea of yours, you revert back to feeling the same pain of rejection that you felt with your parents. You are caught in your parents' trap. That can happen in several ways.

You remain your parents' child. Here's how this works. When you go to your parents' home, do you revert back to the child/teenager who lived there? What things do you do to indicate you are still the child in the family? For example, when my brothers walk into my parents' home, they immediately head for the pantry and the refrigerator to see what there is to eat, even if they've just eaten. "It's a habit," one of them laughs.

Or maybe your parent corrects your behavior—"Don't bite your nails." "Sit up straight." "Where are your manners?" Do you leave resenting your parents for treating you like a child? If you are expecting your parent to meet the unmet emotional needs in your life, you will be disappointed and disillusioned every time you go home. It's time to let others meet your needs and just enjoy your parents for the way they are.

You continue to believe and accept the messages your parents told you as you were growing up. Some may be familiar sayings like, "The early bird catches the worm." Others were either negative or positive statements they repeated frequently. These examples should start you thinking.

» What messages did your parents give you about your physical appearance? "Aren't you getting a little heavy?" "You can't wear that hairstyle in THIS house?" "Nobody's perfect." "It's not what's on the outside, but what's on the inside that counts."

» What messages did your parents give you about your emotions? "Real men don't cry." "Don't let anyone see how you really feel." "Tomorrow is another day." "You will survive!"

» What messages did your parents give you about your performance at school, in a sport, through a club? "Don't disappoint us." "Is that the best you can do?" "Everyone makes mistakes." "I believe in you."

» What messages did your parents give you about your friends? "Your friends are always welcomed here." "Why do you want to be friends with them?" "You're a good friend to have."

You interpreted each message through your needs. These messages, especially those that were repeated frequently, affected how you thought, felt, and behaved as a teenager. The messages may influence your thoughts, feelings, and actions today.

Let's look at Charlie and the message he knew by heart: real men don't cry. As a teenager, Charlie never cried. As an adult, Charlie never cried. He and his wife suffered major setbacks when they tried to have children and couldn't. She cried a lot; he never did. When Charlie buried his parents ten years apart, he was stoic through each funeral. Finally, after almost thirty years of marriage, Charlie cried the morning he found his beautiful, thirteen-year-old Lhasa Apso dead near his favorite chair.

When he woke up his wife to tell her, he kept saying, "Why am I crying over a dog?" They both knew the great bond between

Charlie and his dog. They also knew the tears came for other unexpressed pain. Since that time, Charlie has cried more openly. He no longer believes the message his parents told him that real men don't cry. Charlie's tears now make it easier on his family to see the concern, the pain, and the compassion on the face of their father and know what's in his heart.

How many of the messages that you heard from your parents do you repeat to your teenagers? Are any of these messages the ones you vowed you'd never repeat to your own children? Oops!

LET THE HEALING BEGIN

I have no magic formulas to bring instant healing. These next steps in healing your past are crucial in your relationship with your teenager.

Step 1—Identify the Hurt

As you worked through the emotional gauges in chapter 6, you began to identify areas where you felt your needs were overlooked, short-changed, or ignored. As you worked through this chapter, have you identified specific areas of hurt? Here are several situations that can create hurt in a teenager's life. They are suggested to start you thinking about your own hurt.

- » An overbearing parent who wants total control.
- » An inflexible parent who believes that "if it was good enough for my parents, it's good enough for me!"
- » An absent parent caused by divorce, business travel, or indifference.

156 WHY YOUR KIDS DO WHAT THEY DO

» A parent preoccupied with other siblings, work, older parents, personal interest, or other circumstances.

» A permissive parent who doesn't set any boundaries.

» A parent addicted to alcohol, drugs, gambling, or another destructive behavior.

» Parents dealing with adultery, separation, or divorce.

» An abusive parent.

» An ill parent.

» A sibling who gets all the attention.

» Friends who betray you.

» A romantic breakup.

» A great disappointment.

» A tragic experience.

What was the hurt you faced in your teenage years? Put these hurts into words.

» The person who hurt me the most as a teenager was _____ _____.

» At the time, I felt _____.

» The way I feel about this person today is _____.

» An event that hurt me the most as a teenager was _____ _____.

» At the time, I felt _____.

» The way I feel about this event today is _____.

Step 2—Acknowledge the Pain

Don't skip over this step. Focus on the emotions behind your pain. Identify those feelings. This is a good time to involve someone else in your healing. If you are married, talk to your spouse about the situations and people you identified in step 1 that caused the pain. Ask your spouse to comfort you during this time. Say things that help your spouse know how to respond: "Could you just hold me?" "I need comfort." "I don't need you to talk, just listen." This is not a time for quick-fix suggestions. If you are a single parent, share with a trusted adult who will help you deal with your feelings—not try to fix the hurt.

David Ferguson discusses "grieving the loss" in many of his books. It's a process similar to grieving over the loss of a relationship or the loss of innocence. Grieving lets you consciously free yourself from the damaging hurt of the past. Although the hurt is real today, the reason for the hurt happened a long time ago. By grieving over this hurt, however, you allow yourself to be more open to a future without this pain.

• •

IF YOU DON'T TAKE THE TIME TO GRIEVE, TO WEEP, YOU WILL REMAIN EMOTIONALLY TIED TO THIS PERSON WHO CAUSED THE PAIN.

• •

If you don't take the time to grieve, to weep, you will remain emotionally tied to this person who caused the pain. Maybe that person couldn't give you what they didn't have themselves. Grieving—mourning—in God's healing way, brings about freshness and renewal. Without a chance to grieve, you keep your emotional tank filled with sadness, anger, and hurt—a lot of unhealthy emotions that take the place of healthier emotions.

Think about a hurt that may have happened with your parents. Express your feelings.

» From my dad, I missed _____
_____.
» I felt _____
about not having this experience with my dad.
» I remember a time when I was emotionally hurt by my dad. It involved _____.
» Back then, I felt _____
_____.
» Today, I feel _____
_____.
» From my mom, I missed _____
_____.
» I felt _____
about not having this experience with my mom.
» I remember a time when I was emotionally hurt by my mom. It involved _____.
» Back then, I felt _____
_____.
» Today, I feel _____
_____.

Step 3—Gain Perspective

Involve others in helping you evaluate your hurt and your feelings. Ask others to help you see a different perspective. Look at the experiences through different eyes.

» Talk to your siblings about the events that caused you pain. Do older siblings know more of the story? Did they experience similar feelings?

» A trusted family friend or neighbor of your family may be able to give you a new perspective. Do they know of events that were happening to your parents that you didn't notice or understand? Did your parents talk to this person and share their feelings about the event? How did your parents describe you to others? What were your parents' feelings about you?

» You may even get a new perspective from your parents. Make a list of actions that you saw as hurtful. (You never came to my ball games. You missed my high school graduation. You always expected me to get an A.) Beside each hurt, write a possible defense your parent gave at the time or might give now. (You missed my graduation because you had an emergency business deal out of town that couldn't wait.) Show the list to your parent, asking the parent if this is a true picture of the situation. Listen to the other side of the story—not from a child's point of view but from an adult's viewpoint. Since you now have children, does your parents' explanation make more sense?

» Someone who could help me gain perspective is _____
_____.

» I want to ask this person about _____
_____.

» I believe I could ask my parent about _____
_____.

Step 4—Forgive and Be Forgiven

Forgive first. Don't play the blame game; refuse to continue blaming someone who has hurt you. Because God has forgiven you, you can forgive others. Forgiveness is a choice. You choose to forgive, even though the feelings of pain remain. Forgiving someone who has hurt you gives you freedom and strength.

» You can forgive before the person who hurt you asks for forgiveness.
» You can forgive, knowing the person who hurt you may never change their damaging behavior.
» You can forgive, even when your natural inclination would be revenge.

One way to frame your forgiveness to a parent is to share your pain directly with the parent, not in an accusatory manner, but in a way that states the facts. For example, you might say, "When I was a teenager, I was hurt by the times you came home so late that I never got to see you. It felt like you were avoiding me or didn't like me. I'm forgiving you for that hurt because I want to get on with my life."

If you don't think you can talk directly to your parent without saying the wrong thing, record your message. State how you felt about a specific action or lack of action by your parent. State how this has hurt you and your desire to let it go. Then, state your forgiveness. By making the recording, you have the chance to edit out comments that sound too harsh or judgmental. You can still play the recording for your parent and discuss it.

You could also write a letter to your parent. Identify the specific incident, or express the general hurt you felt. In the letter, state that you are choosing to forgive your parent in order to heal and to change the relationship with your own children. Writing such a letter comforts you. If you can deliver the letter in person and discuss it, that will bring additional healing, especially when you emphasize that you are not placing blame; you're just trying to understand and forgive. If your parent has died, the letter writing offers a natural release of the built-up unexpressed pain.

You can also write a letter and not deliver it. Let the feelings you express be the way to release your hurt and pain.

» A hurt I am willing to forgive is _____
_____.

» I am willing to talk to _____
about this.

» The way I will do it is to _____
_____.

Be forgiven. Perhaps, you need to ask for forgiveness from your parents. Your unmet needs may have been the motivation behind your behavior, but that behavior may have been destructive in your relationship with your parents. Begin by asking God to forgive your sin. Rejoice in His forgiveness. Next, ask for your parents' forgiveness. You could use any of the ideas suggested above.

This is not the time to ask for your teenager's forgiveness about your past selfishness and shortcomings. I'll help you deal with that relationship in the next chapter. First, ask for forgiveness from your family.

➤ A hurt I realize I have caused is _____

_____.

➤ I am willing to ask forgiveness from _____

_____.

➤ The way I will do it is to _____

_____.

Step 5—Grow from Your Experience.

Build off the sense of healing that you experience. Here are several things to help you continue to heal as you grow.

How can you meet the needs of your parents today? Think of a way to meet a need before either of them asks. Perhaps the need is physical in nature, like changing lightbulbs or taking care of the lawn. If possible, try to focus on an emotional need. Maybe your parents need to know they are appreciated. Maybe they would like a little attention.

➤ A need I see in my mom's life is _____

_____.

➤ I can meet that need by _____

_____.

» A need I see in my dad's life is _____

_____.

» I can meet that need by _____

_____.

From this day, build on the positive things you remember.

» Things my dad did right:
» Things my mom did right:

After going through this process, you may still feel that very little healing has occurred. It may be time to seek professional help. Look at a professional as a copilot, guiding you through this tricky emotional stuff. You are not admitting defeat by going to a counselor. Instead, you are acknowledging that God has gifted others with the ability to give you perspective and guidance. You should particularly seek professional counseling if you are depressed and see no hope or if you are concerned that you might endanger others because of your anger and pain.

Step 6—Thank Significant Others

During your teen years, some people did things right. These may have been siblings, other family members, significant adults like coaches, neighbors, teachers, youth workers, or even older peers who offered encouragement and guidance. Pause to reflect on the thanks you owe other people. These people may have stepped up and met your needs in a healthy way. After working through this final section, you might want to drop a note of appreciation to those whom you remember.

➤ When I was with _____.
 I always felt _____.
 I am grateful for _____
 _____.

➤ When I was with _____.
 I always felt _____.
 I am grateful for _____
 _____.

➤ When I was with _____.
 I always felt _____.
 I am grateful for _____
 _____.

In the next chapter, you will see how to get your own needs met and what you can do about the future.

CHAPTER 8

LOOKING TO THE FUTURE

Congratulations on getting this far in the "Understanding Yourself" portion of the book. You have looked at your past and identified the unmet needs that motivated your past behavior. I know it's tough to face these painful memories, but your efforts will pay off in the future. The next step is to find ways to get your needs met, so you can meet the needs of your teenager.

GETTING YOUR NEEDS MET

Review the gauges and needs you checked at the end of chapter 6. Now that you know what your present needs are, here are some ideas for getting those needs met.

Be aware that it's okay to admit that you need others. Some people think admitting you have needs means admitting you are weak or unable to take care of yourself. It doesn't. It takes great courage and vulnerability to share with someone what you need. Learn how to be vulnerable, transparent, and open with those you love who want to love you. As you build on already healthy, strong relationships, you will find many ways that others can meet your needs.

Be aware of letting others know your needs. God made us to need one another. It's okay to ask others for help. The first person you can turn to is your spouse, but don't expect your spouse to read your mind and figure out your needs. Lovingly share your needs in such a way that doesn't attack the other person. It may be your spouse's weakness that leaves you feeling needy, but you gain nothing by accusing that person. Express your need in a loving, factual way. To gain respect from your spouse, which of the following remarks do you think will work the best?

#1—"You never listen to my point of view! Why is your way always the best way? You know I have some pretty good ideas too. But you never give me a chance to express them."

#2—"Honey, I'm really struggling with an issue. I don't feel like my ideas and opinions are very important to you. When there's a decision involving the house or the car or the children, I feel left out when you make a decision without me. I'm hurt by being ignored. Will you please include me on these decisions in the future?"

If you are a single parent, you can look to other family members and close friends to meet your needs. If your relationship with your parents is strong and healthy, look to them for help. Best friends, siblings, your church family, and even an extended family of emotionally healthy adults can help meet your needs if they know what you need. For married couples who may not meet one another's needs all the time, these are also healthy options.

Beware of looking for someone to meet your needs who is inappropriate. Just like the teenager with unmet needs, you might find yourself caught up in a situation where you get your needs met in an unhealthy way. For example, if you need to feel loved and do not get love at home, you may look to someone of the opposite sex at work. Your vulnerability may lead you to make unwise choices. Don't justify any destructive behavior by claiming it's the way you can get your needs met.

Beware of expecting your teenager to meet your needs. Teenagers already deal with emotional overload. Until they get emotionally healthy and more mature, they depend on you to meet their needs—not the other way around. They cannot adequately meet your needs until they become adults, operating from an adult emotional age. Unfortunately, some parents abuse their teenager's willingness to listen by griping about neglect, inattention, loneliness, or lack of appreciation.

• •

EVERYONE HAS NEEDS. THE NUMBER, INTENSITY, AND PRIORITY OF THESE NEEDS VARY FROM PERSON TO PERSON.

• •

Beware of whining, acting like a child, expecting others to "discover" your needs, selfishness, or "pity parties." Admitting you have needs is not whining. Whiners complain without seeking or accepting solutions. Admitting you have needs is not childish. Childishness is sulking and pouting, hoping someone will eventually figure out what's wrong with you. Admitting you have needs is not selfishness. Selfishness is attacking and blaming others without being truthful and up-front. Admitting you have needs is not having a pity party where everyone should feel sorry for you. Everyone has needs. The number, intensity, and priority of these needs vary from person to person.

» A need I feel in my life is _____
_____.

» The person I will ask to meet this need is _____
_____.

» I will try to share my need in this way _____
_____.

Be aware of how you can meet others' needs. I've already explained how you can't meet another's needs when you are missing that need in your life; you cannot give what you do not have. I hope you see that there are many ways to get your needs met. As your needs are met, it's a natural process that you give to others. There is great warmth and comfort in giving of yourself to others. When your emotional tank is full, it's time to start filling the emotional tank of your teenager.

Beware of feelings that may make it difficult to meet your teenager's needs. Don't be afraid of your teenager. Underneath that attitude, clothing, loud music, and hair is a hurting teenager waiting to soak up love, respect, attention, and nurture like a sponge. Their attitudes are really shields deflecting the painful reality of life. Their clothing and hair are part of the search for individuality. The loud music and strange behaviors affirm that they are still alive. Push past the discomfort of your teenager's strange world, and find the reward of helping your teen discover their unlimited potential.

ABCs FOR THE FUTURE

I hope you are beginning to heal from the hurts of past unmet needs. As you share your present needs, I pray that you will allow others to meet those needs. Let's now turn to the future. The following ABCs present things you can do to prepare for meeting the needs of your teenager. You may want to return to this checklist often to stay balanced as you meet your teen's needs.

Adjust Your Attitude

As you understand the reasons behind your teenager's behavior, you can move from an attitude of frustration and fear to an attitude of confidence. Instead of operating from the point of view that always punishes, you become proactive by meeting your teenager's needs and hopefully halting negative behavior before it starts.

See your teenager as a gift from God. If you enjoy writing, keep a list of positive qualities you notice each day. Read the list on days when parenting a teenager gets rough. Appreciate what your teenager does right; ignore the rest, if possible.

Sally came home one day with her midterm report card in hand. Before giving it to her mother, Sally listed all the reasons why her grades weren't up to what her parents expected. She even talked about specific things she planned to do to correct the low scores. In other words, by the time Sally handed her midterm report card to her mom, there wasn't much left for mom to say. After looking at the report, however, mom did comment on the fact that all of Sally's teachers gave her excellent marks for conduct and participation. By the end of the quarter, Sally had brought her grades up, as promised. A couple of years later, Sally retold the story to a friend and expressed how grateful she was that her mom saw something good in her—instead of her poor grades.

Bear Responsibility for Past Mistakes

At an appropriate time, share with your teenager what you are reading and learning about unmet needs. Apologize to your teenager and express your desire to change. For example, you might say something like, "I have been wrong in not paying attention to you. Please forgive me. I want to do better. I was wondering if you would like to do something together this week?" or, "I didn't know how to be a parent. I've never been the parent of a fourteen-year-old son, but I'm going to try harder. Will you work with me?" Whatever you do, don't blame others for what has been missing in your teenager's life. Rather than making excuses, try to be upbeat and positive when you share your desire to meet your teenager's needs.

You may need to repeat this process several times as you discover other needs in your teen's life that have been neglected. As you begin to change the way you relate to your teenager (using the actions suggested in chapter 9), your teen may actually come to you and ask what's going on. What a great time to share what you are hoping to do!

• •

AS YOU BEGIN TO CHANGE THE WAY YOU RELATE TO YOUR TEENAGER (USING THE ACTIONS SUGGESTED IN CHAPTER 9), YOUR TEEN MAY ACTUALLY COME TO YOU AND ASK WHAT'S GOING ON. WHAT A GREAT TIME TO SHARE WHAT YOU ARE HOPING TO DO!

• •

Comfort Your Teenager

Working through your own journey of unmet needs showed you the value of being comforted. You also saw how not being comforted can be painful and hurtful. If you have not been comforted in the past, you may not know how to comfort others, especially a stricken teenager. You can begin with words of comfort. Why do these sentences fail to give comfort?

"You're not the only teenager who's had this experience."

"This is not going to kill you."

"Why is this such a big deal?"

"How do you think I feel? I have some feelings too."

"Get a life! You always dwell on the negative stuff."

Pain, hurt, rejection, frustration, disappointment, confusion, denial, losing out, broken relationships, shattered dreams, anger, fear, and isolation—these intense emotions rip away at the hearts and souls of teenagers. Comforting a teen requires empathy, gentleness, and affection. Even when a teenager stiffly rejects hugs, a hand on the shoulder or a brief back rub can still be a comforting touch. Some teenagers who have not been exposed to comforting words and gestures may enjoy the comforting. Others who are uncomfortable with touching may take a little longer. You also want to weigh how affectionate to be with a teenager based on the comfort level of your teenager with that quickly changing body. Younger teens are particularly self-conscious and uncomfortable being close to others.

Think of a time when you were really hurting. What words helped you heal? What words of comfort does your teenager need? It may take a while before your teen reveals the pain or hurt happening in his or her life. This means you must pay attention to a vocal teenager who becomes quiet, a restless teenager who becomes listless, or an upbeat teenager who acts depressed. For example, your older son may not be willing to admit how hurt he is about breaking up with his girlfriend. Your daughter may not know how to explain her embarrassment at changing in the girls' locker room at school.

Comforting words sound like this:
» "I know this is hurting you."
» "I'm so sad that you have to feel this way."
» "I'm going to stay with you through this. I'm here for you."
» "I'm sorry you've had this experience."
» "How can I help? I love you and want to support you."

Your first experience in comforting your teenager may feel awkward, but the more you do it, the better it will be accepted.

Discover the Uniqueness of Each Child

Many children complain, "My parents like my brother/sister better!" Actually, I know many parents want to treat their children equally, but there is nothing equal about the situations. The firstborn child ends up being the one nervous moms and dads learn to parent. Finances may be tighter. Grandparents will be watching (and maybe participating) more closely with the first child. Children born later arrive in a different financial climate—maybe even a different neighborhood. Grandparents may or may not be as involved, depending on their health and distance.

• •

NOTE THE INDIVIDUALITY OF YOUR CHILDREN. DEAL WITH EACH TEENAGER BASED ON THAT TEENAGER'S STRENGTHS AND WEAKNESSES.

• •

Note the individuality of your children. Deal with each teenager based on that teenager's strengths and weaknesses. Be especially careful not to project one teenager's negative characteristics onto another child who doesn't have the same emotional makeup. Appreciate the differences in your children.

Energize Your Parenting Skills

You already know you'll never win the "Perfect Parent Award." So try to be a really great parent! Reading books like this one, attending seminars, talking with other parents of teenagers, and learning how they face different situations all bring new life and energy to the seemingly endless years of parenting a teenager.

Find Constructive Ways to Vent Frustrations

When you are hurting or angry or tired, call a good friend to listen, go for a walk, or bang around in the kitchen or a workshop. Never allow yourself to use these behaviors in any situation:

➤ Abusive behavior or language—If you feel you may lose control or are afraid you will hit your teenager or use language that puts the teenager down, talk to someone (a trusted friend, counselor, or another parent) who can help you get perspective and control.

➤ Playing favorites—Although you won't be treating each teen the same, be careful not to favor one over the other. The favorite teen feels as much pressure as the teen who receives little attention and is trying to get it.

➤ Inconsistent expectations—Understanding a parent is difficult enough for a young person, but not having a consistent foundation confuses the teenager even more. Continually check that what you say with your mouth is reflected in what you live with your life. Let your teenager know what your values are; then, live these values in front of your teen.

Give Attention to Your Marriage

Raising teenagers can strain a marriage. The different ways you and your spouse were parented become even more obvious during these years of parenting a teenager. But remember: you need each other. Spend time with your spouse—dinner and a movie, a weekend retreat, or a marriage conference at your church. Plan to do something every month that involves just the two of you. Keeping your marriage healthy is a tough assignment, but when that last teenager leaves home, you and your spouse still want to have something to talk about over dinner. Hopefully, you have included your spouse in this quest to understand your teenager. This gives you many areas to discuss as you work together to help your teenager.

If you are a single parent, your task is harder but not impossible. You don't have a soulmate to rely on for emotional and physical support. Enlist a same-sex person who can be a friend, mentor, or confidante—someone who can give perspective and support. Even though you may have the opportunity to marry during your teenager's developing years, weigh the need to stay focused on your teenager for this brief amount of time rather than get involved in a new relationship. Adult relationship development takes time, energy, and emotional investment that you need to devote to getting your teenager on track and headed into the future in a healthy manner. A dating parent also makes it difficult for their teenager to understand a parent's sexuality at a time when they are struggling with their own.

If you currently live in a blended family, then you may already be dealing with the difficult task of raising a teenager amid new relationships in the household. If you have been a blended family prior to your teenager's adolescence, the impact may not be as great. If you decide to get married during your teenager's adolescence, however, all statistics point to this being a traumatic time for your teenager. Consider seeking professional guidance in getting everyone in the family working on the same page.

Give Unconditional Love

Although I've discussed the necessity of showing unconditional love in meeting the needs of teenagers, I must underscore its importance here. In evaluating your own teenage years, you've seen how conditional love damages and even destroys relationships. Unconditional love accepts the person today—this hour—right now. He is your son; she is your daughter. You gave that teenager a chance at life through birth, adoption, or guardianship. Apart from God, you are the one true source of unconditional love for that teenager.

● ●

UNCONDITIONAL LOVE ACCEPTS THE PERSON TODAY—THIS HOUR—RIGHT NOW. HE IS YOUR SON; SHE IS YOUR DAUGHTER.

● ●

Take a practical look at unconditional love by using this exercise based on 1 Corinthians 13:4-8:

Love is patient, love is kind. It does not envy, it does not boast, it is not proud. It is not rude, it is not self-seeking, it is not easily angered, it keeps no record of wrongs. Love does not delight in evil but rejoices with the truth. It always protects, always trusts, always hopes, always perseveres. Love never fails.

It's time to move on to chapter 9 where you will find numerous specific ideas for meeting each of the needs listed. Are you ready to tackle the task of meeting your teen's needs? Then, let's go!

PART 3

KNOWING AND LOVING EACH OTHER

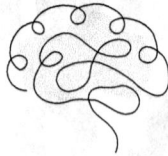

CHAPTER 9

ACTIONS AND ATTITUDES THAT SPEAK LOUDER THAN WORDS

S tuart's grandfather died suddenly. Before his death, Stuart's grandfather often took Stuart fishing, to the movies, or out to eat good, old-fashioned barbecue. Several weeks after the funeral, Stuart and a couple of his buddies trashed the boys' locker room at school. He was suspended for a week.

What would you do? Would you do something different than what you would have done before reading this book? I hope so. I've tried to show you that the way to change a teenager's behavior is to meet his or her needs not just react to the behavior. As you think about Stuart's situation, apply the differences between this life-giving way of relating to your teenagers with the way many parents relate to teens.

Many Parents Today . . .	Revolutionary Relationship Parents . . .
focus on the problem behavior	look beyond the behavior to the motivation
use punishment as the only way to change the behavior	meet a need to correct the attitude behind the behavior
blame others for the problem (peers, society, media, other parents, work)	accept responsibility for unmet needs and act to meet the need
operate from frustration	operate from confidence
try to change the teenager when the teenager sees no need to change	offer the teenager a reason to change as needs are met
love conditionally ("I'll love you if you . . .")	love unconditionally ("I love you because . . .")
spend time and energy worrying about your teenager	spend time and energy meeting needs of your teenager
suffer parenting burn-out	understand your teenager's behavior
feel uncomfortable because you don't relate to the teenager on a meaningful level	feel comfortable with your teenager as deeper relationship develops

MANY PARENTS TODAY

The number one thing teenagers want is happiness. And they're reasonably satisfied to find that happiness in ways most parents don't consider. Teenagers see financial, personal, or career success as separate goals—not what will make them happy.[39]

---

39 "The 'One Thing' Teens Want," *Youthworker*, March/April 1998, 17 (quoting *USA Today*, December 9, 1997).

Teenagers list other wants that may surprise parents. A survey of teenagers between the ages of twelve and seventeen for a report titled "Kids These Days: What Americans Really Think about the Next Generation," found that:

» **Teenagers want to be disciplined.** They aren't. Half the parents admit that they fail to discipline their teenagers when they should. One-third of the teenagers agreed. Teenagers want encouragement and compliments. Sixty-five percent say they hear positive words from adults nearly every day.[40]

» **Teenagers want more attention.** Almost half of those polled said they wanted more guidance and attention from adults. Another study shows that parents spend an average of thirty-nine minutes a week in meaningful conversation with their children.[41] Even if parents count the essential actions (feeding, clothing, reading to, and playing) with children from birth through adolescence, the time is still limited. Employed women spend six and a half hours a week in undivided child care; non-employed women spend six hours more. Unemployed and employed men give about the same time of two and a half hours per week.[42]

» **Teenagers want parents' help in making decisions about their future.** A Gallup Youth Survey of thirteen- to seventeen-year-olds reported the influence of parents on teenagers' decisions. Parents had the greatest impact on whether or not the teenager attended college (77 percent), whether

40 "Adults Don't Approve of Kids," *Youthworker*, September/October 1997, 16 (from *San Antonio Express-News*, June 27, 1997).
41 "It's Lonely at the Tube," *Youthworker Update*, November 1995, 6 *(Denver Post*, August 22, 1995).
42 Laura Shapiro, "The Myth of Quality Time," *Newsweek*, May 12, 1997, 65.

or not to attend religious services (70 percent), whether or not to do homework (68 percent), and what job or career plans should be considered (63 percent).[43]

WHAT TEENAGERS NEED—GETTING STARTED

You learned about the five emotional gauges (NEEDS) in chapter 2. Now you'll discover specific actions and attitudes you can take to meet your teenager's needs and keep gauges balanced. To put these actions and attitudes into effect, follow these steps.

Step 1: Start With a New Way of Thinking

Approach your teenager and your teenager's behavior from a new perspective. Look for the motivation behind the behavior. That doesn't mean you ignore the behavior. Discipline may be needed in the form of natural consequences or specific punishment. But operate from a proactive, preventative role as you love, encourage, nurture, and respect your teenager into more positive behavior.

Step 2: Focus on One Gauge at a Time

Use the "Needs Evaluation" worksheet in chapter 2 to determine your teenager's most pressing needs. If you have not included your teenager in this process to this point, ask him or her to use the survey as a way to begin a conversation about your actions. Perhaps you already know your teenager's number one need. Focus on that need for the next few weeks.

---

43 *Emerging Trends*, September 1997, www.emergeonline.com/trends.

Step 3: Model What You Are Trying to Do

Model the unconditional love that you know is so important. Don't be bullied by a teenager who may resist your initial actions. After all, your new behavior and attitude may seem a little suspicious. Don't be surprised if your teenager decides to test you to see how sincere you are. They want to know if you are going to respect their privacy, or if this is just a phase. They may say or do things to get you to react in your old pattern of behavior. They may act out in other ways to see if you really mean, "I'm going to love you, no matter what." Accept this period of testing as normal.

Step 4: Be Open About Why You Are Making These Changes

Explain that you don't want to repeat the problems you experienced as a teenager when people you counted on didn't meet your needs. Invite your teenager to join you as a partner. Challenge your teenager to give the experience a "test run" of six months.

Step 5: Start Now

It's never too late. Stay focused on your goal. Pursue God with all your heart for His wisdom, strength, and guidance. God has a good, pleasing, and perfect will for your kids and family.

WHAT TEENAGERS NEED—ACTIONS AND ATTITUDES

Under each gauge are the basic needs. Then, you'll find a list of actions and attitudes to use in meeting each need. Some actions can be implemented quickly; others will take time to develop. Use these next few pages as a workbook. Write in the margins other actions that come to mind as you consider these. Star or circle the actions you plan to take. You might even place a date next to an action as a time frame when you hope to see a change in your teenager's behavior. Record Bible verses or phrases that come to mind as a reminder that God is in this with you.

The Noticed Gauge

"I need focused *attention*."

1) Pay attention when your teenager is talking. Watch body language and facial expressions for clues about your teenager's feelings.

   » Put down your phone, stop watching TV, or turn down the volume. Remove all distractions.

   » Ask open-ended questions, "Why did your coach take Pete out of the game early?" "What did you talk about in world history class today?"

   » Say, "I'm available." Let your teenager know you are always available—24/7—if they need a listening ear. Even if their timing to talk may not be convenient for you as a parent, give them a time frame. ("I'll be through in ten minutes. I want to talk with you.")

2) Enter the world of your teenager. Look at events and situations from the teenager's point of view.

   » Go to school-sponsored events. Host a small group of students from your church in your home or chaperone a youth retreat or camp (with your teenager's permission).

   » Offer to take a group of younger teenagers out for pizza and let them sit at another table. Listen to their conversations while you are driving. Teenagers forget that the driver has ears!

» Watch your teenager play video games and discuss the strategy, scoring, etc., and discuss why they enjoy playing it so much.

» Listen to and discuss the songs your teenager prefers. This is easy to do in a car. Don't condemn the music. Try to understand why they like certain songs. Ask your teenager how it makes them feel or what message they hear in the song. Remember: you once liked the "beat" to or "feel" of certain songs growing up, even though you didn't grasp the full impact of the words.

» Work on homework together. Show your teenager the study hacks you learned. Get them to explain the subject to you, so you can help. (Usually, in the explanation, they will suddenly understand the problem.) Don't be a "know-it-all"; you might learn something too.

3) Do something special with your teenager.

» Spend time alone with each child in your family. Plan a regular (weekly, monthly, bimonthly) "date" if possible.

» Brainstorm a list of activities to do with your teenager. Together, select several and write these on the family calendar.

» Let your teenager teach you something (how to play a video game, edit a video, play the guitar or piano).

» Explore new places with your teenager (a vintage clothing store, a new bike trail).

4) Indicate that you think about your teenager during the day. Say things like, "I thought about what you said. . . ." "I saw something today that reminded me of you." "A friend at work expressed the same opinion you had about. . . ."

5) Occasionally invite the teenager into your world (for lunch or on an interesting business trip).

6) Eat dinner as a family at least three days a week. Make it a priority.

7) Always greet your teenager in the morning, when returning home, or when your teenager walks into a room.

"I am *respected* as a person."

1) Speak with respect.

   ⟫ Avoid demeaning statements, insults, or derogatory names for your teenager.

   ⟫ Avoid teasing of any kind.

   ⟫ Apologize when you are wrong or when you have hurt your teenager through a misunderstanding, unkind words, unfair discipline, or an incorrect assumption.

   ⟫ Praise the way your teenager handles a situation, especially a problem.

   ⟫ Don't ask prying questions.

   ⟫ If you must correct your teenager, do it privately in a calm tone of voice.

2) Act with honor and respect toward your teenager.

   ⟫ Respect your teenager's time by being on time. If you pick them up at school or need to get them to an appointment, don't be late.

   ⟫ Be courteous and use your "company" manners with family members. Say "please" and "thank you."

   ⟫ Knock before entering your teenager's room or the bathroom when the door is closed. Wait for a response.

» Model the behavior you want from your teenager: speak in a softer voice, let your teenager know where you are going and the time you will return, and leave a note or send them a text when you are not going to be home and the time you will be back home.

3) Respect your teenager's desire for independence.

» Consult with your teenager before committing his or her time to a specific activity (babysitting, a neighbor's yard work, a project at church, or a youth activity).

» Ask for your teenager's advice or opinion, especially if the decision impacts the teenager (where to vacation, changing schools, how to spend spring break).

» Consider the teenager's need for privacy. If your teenager shares a room with a sibling, figure out a way to give the teenager personal space.

» Allow your teenager to have personal time alone with the door shut.

» Understand when your teenager doesn't want to be around you in public; it's not a personal thing but an independence issue.

4) See your teenager's friends as people whom God loves. Talk to them as teenagers who might be hurting and need someone to listen. Don't stereotype them as weird, even if they are.

"I am *valued* for who I am."

1) Value your teenager's positive qualities.

» Frequently say, "I think you're an amazing person because..." with specific reasons.

➤ Applaud your teenager for standing by their morals or showing good character, especially in the face of peer pressure. Slip a note under their bedroom door or send a text expressing your admiration.

➤ Support your teenager's healthy, constructive decisions.

➤ Talk to your teenager about others' admirable qualities and why you admire them.

➤ Get in the habit of sincerely complimenting your teenager at least once a day. Compliment your teenager's character and other qualities you admire.

➤ Notice and acknowledge immediately something the teenager does that is positive.

➤ State how your teenager is a valuable part of the family.

2) Share your admiration for your teenager with others.

➤ Talk about your teenager's positive qualities to others within the teenager's hearing. Be sincere—not boastful.

➤ Be positive in what you say about your teenager to others.

"I am *appreciated* for what I do."

1) State your appreciation.

➤ Verbally thank your teenager for completing a task, even if it's a regular chore.

➤ Stop expecting your teenager to figure out what needs to be done. Instead, be specific in asking for help and stating a time limit.

➤ Volunteer (with the teenager's permission) to chaperone youth events at school or church. Watch and listen to other teenagers during the event. Afterward, compliment your teenager for something good you saw your teenager do.

» Praise your teenager in front of others in a pleasant, unembarrassing way.

» Catch your teenager doing something right and verbally praise him.

2) Show your appreciation.

» Express your gratitude for your teenager's kindness in a way your teenager will appreciate (a touch, a hug, a thank-you note stuck on the mirror, a flower, or a funny card in an unexpected place like their math book).

» Notice what your teenager collects. Occasionally surprise them with a "thank-you" item for their collection.

» Learn what your teenager likes (candy bar, favorite drink, type of gum). Occasionally surprise them with the item as a gesture of appreciation.

» Make a list of the positive qualities about your teenager. Read the list, especially when times are rough.

» Write a prayer thanking God for your teenager.

» Look for things to experience with your teenager (a movie, a starry night, a 5K race).

3) Teach appreciation to your teenager.

» Regularly have a "topic of the day" (news, sports, music, a value) at dinner. Agree to disagree with laughter.

» Notice and express your appreciation for God's creation (a beautiful sunset, a rainbow, a new baby).

The Encouragement Gauge

"I need to be *nurtured* as I reach for my dreams."

1) Cultivate the practical side of helping your teenager.

» Listen to what your teenager struggles with and offer physical, emotional, financial, or spiritual support, as appropriate.

» Provide financial stability. Don't talk about how poor you are or what you don't have. Teach them to have an abundance mindset versus a scarcity mindset.

» Involve your teenager in a project that helps others in order to learn the value of service.

» Demonstrate good financial skills by making and keeping a budget, paying off bills, using credit cards responsibly by paying them off each month, and getting estimates for large projects.

» Teach your teenager how to balance a checkbook, shop for the best buys, or use an ATM or banking apps. By the ninth grade, a teenager should have a checking account. Most banks don't charge a monthly fee if the parents have an account in the same bank.

» Go with a teenager to look at colleges. Plan a "college tour" during the summer before their junior or senior year.

» Teach life skills—how to do laundry, how to plan an event, how to shop for and cook a meal, how to iron a shirt, or how to tie a tie.

» Involve your teenager in making decisions by weighing the pros and cons, even if the decision does not directly affect your teenager.

2) Help dreams become a reality.

» Help your teenager define a life goal.

» Help your teenager set goals for the future: going to college, buying a car, or paying for a senior trip.

- Allow your teenager to work at a variety of jobs or volunteer in the church or other organizations to see what they enjoy and find most rewarding.
- Don't dismiss or discourage your teenager's dreams. Teenagers go from "What I want to be when I grow up" to "How do I get to what I want to be?" Expose them to personality and strength assessments to help them find their "strength zone."
- Assure your teenager of your commitment to them through the long haul.
- Invite engaging adults with a variety of interests into your home to talk about their interests and expose the teenager to other options in life.
- Always hold out hope.

"I need to be *supported* when I feel like giving up."
1) Offer physical support.
- Be action-oriented in supporting your teenager. Do it all the time.
- Post sticky notes with encouraging messages in surprising places—in a school book, in their shoes, on their pillow. Send a text with a supportive message or Bible verses.
- Walk with your teenager through the normal consequences of poor decisions. Help them to understand how to learn from their mistakes and commit to becoming a person of character.
- Celebrate little victories like a completed term paper, the end of final exams, a hard test, or making the team

by fixing their favorite dinner, going out to their favorite restaurant, or doing something your teenager really enjoys.

➤ Do your teenager's regular chores as a way to help out during a difficult time.

2) Offer emotional support.

➤ Pray for your teenager daily. Tell your teenager you are praying for a specific situation or event. Pray with your teenager in the car (with your eyes open, of course) or over the phone.

➤ Encourage your teenager to keep a journal of feelings, ideas, and statements of anger. Never pry into this journal.

➤ Notice times of high stress (at midterms, during exams, SAT test days, a family illness), and be especially encouraging and upbeat.

➤ Never criticize your teenager in front of others, especially their peers.

The Empathy Gauge

"I need to receive *comfort* when I experience pain, sorrow, or despair."

1) Focus on the feelings of your teenager.

➤ Say things that show you care. ("Wow! It sounds like you had a rough day." "I know that was difficult." "I hurt with you.")

➤ Avoid dismissive phrases: "You'll get over it." "No one ever died of a broken heart." "Don't make this such a big deal!"

➤ Don't immediately place blame. Listen or ask questions to get the whole story.

» Tell your teenager it's okay to cry. Cry with your teenager, but don't use your tears to manipulate your teenager.

» Recognize that teenagers have feelings, too, even when they can't express them. You might ask, "Does this make you angry?" "I'd be frustrated; aren't you?"

» Be aware of how devastating these events can be in a teenager's life: rejection, disappointment, a physical illness that isolates the teenager, stress (real or imagined), unemployment (firing), the death of a person (grandparent, favorite relative, another teenager), the death of a pet, a national or local tragedy, parents' divorce, a move, or any broken relationship.

» Apologize for bringing sorrow and pain into a teenager's life for whatever reason—divorce (even if it happened when the teenager was young), a business move that uproots a teenager, having to care for an elderly parent, or whatever the stress.

2) Help your teenager deal with the pain, hurt, or crisis.

» Listen without offering a solution. (Dads, you don't have to solve the problem every time.)

» Hug your teenager during a rough time, put a hand on her arm, or put your arm around his shoulder to show your concern.

» Cheer up a discouraged teenager by spending time together in an activity that the teenager enjoys—a movie and a pizza, a ball game, miniature golfing, or playing a computer game.

3) Apologize when you are wrong.
4) Don't talk about your bad day or your bad experience unless your teenager asks.
5) Make your teenager's friends feel comfortable in your home. Hang around the kitchen while the friends are there; they always want to eat! If they stay in the den, bring them soft drinks and popcorn.

The Direction Gauge

"I need to feel a sense of *significance and purpose* in my life."
1) View your teenager as important.
   ›› Find out what makes your teenager feel significant—verbal or written praise, praise shared with others about your teenager, encouragement on a task, working with your teenager on the task—whatever it is, commit to doing it.
   ›› Practice seeing life from your teenager's perspective.
   ›› Write or type your teenager's activities on the family calendar.
   ›› Remember dates of significant events—graduations, getting the learner's license and driver's license, SAT test days, exams, senior prom, awards ceremonies, and games.
   ›› Attend games, recitals, concerts, award programs, school dramas, or church events—any and all activities that involve your teenager.
   ›› Introduce your teenager to a variety of opportunities and situations. Support a teenager's desire to try out for a team or to try drama or karate. Expose them to a variety of entertainment, from live theater to art exhibitions. Make

a list of all the events in your area and plan with your teenager to do something different each month for a year.

➤➤ Pray for your teenager's strengths and weaknesses, gifts and abilities, and future mate. Let your teenager "catch you" in your time alone with God.

2) Teach your teenager about what's really important in life, leadership, and relationships.

➤➤ Lead your family in a home Bible study. Talk about the promises in the Bible, the passages on love, the characteristics of God, the miracles of Jesus, the Proverbs, and what we mean to God.

➤➤ Involve your teenager in opportunities to see the servant side of life. For example, send your teenager on youth mission trips. Do a mission project as a family (serve in a local soup kitchen, participate in an Angel Tree, volunteer at a local hospital or inner city recreation center, or build a Habitat house together).

➤➤ Talk about news stories, events, and situations where other people care for, give to, and serve others.

➤➤ Model that others are significant by treating everyone with respect and kindness.

➤➤ Encourage your teenager's desire to make a difference in life.

The Security Gauge

"I need to feel physical *security.*"

1) Offer physical safety.

➤➤ Create a physically secure, safe home.

➤ Offer to work with school officials, law enforcement, other parents, and neighbors to make your teenager's school and neighborhood safe. Find out what safety precautions are in place at your teenager's school.

➤ Treat your teenager in a healthy manner. Never threaten, never hit, and never throw anything at your teenager.

➤ Acknowledge their fears. Listen as your teenager talks about these fears.

➤ Tell your teenager to call you to be picked up anytime they are feeling uncomfortable or put in dangerous situations—no matter the time, place, or circumstances— no questions asked! If this is not practical, offer to get someone else to pick them up.

2) Establish and defend family values.

➤ Clarify family values, standards, and expectations about things like curfew, driving, riding with another teenage driver, clothing, chores, language, friends in the teenager's bedroom, movies, videos, music, parties, spending money, outside school activities, and other areas of your teenager's life. Do not assume that your teenager knows your position on any of these. The values and expectations are to serve as guideposts to direct them and guardrails to protect them.

➤ Renegotiate family standards and expectations frequently, especially as the teenager becomes older and shows they can be trusted. Tell your teenager you are willing to talk about these issues at any time.

➤ Discuss how to set personal boundaries. Let your teenager know what boundaries you place in your life. (For example, if you travel, what restrictions do you place on yourself? How do you decide what movies to see? What activities do you do or not do away from the family?)

» Communicate assurance of your marriage commitment to your spouse. Live out this commitment by the way you and your spouse treat one another.

» Keep your disagreements with your spouse between the two of you. Don't involve the teenagers either as messengers or pawns. Don't manipulate your teenager into taking sides in an argument with your spouse.

» If you are single, put your teenager's needs first. Consider waiting until your teenager has become an adult before remarrying.

» Defend your teenager's boundaries when others try to violate them. Tell your teenager, "Make me the bad guy!" That way, your teenager can say, "My dad will explode if I do that."

» Demonstrate a desire to trust God, especially in times of uncertainty or danger.

» Hold regular family meetings where everyone has a voice, especially in areas affecting your teenager (vacations, a move to another city, or schedule changes).

» If you can't be home when your teenager gets home, make a thirty-second phone call a couple of times during the afternoon to let your teenager know you care. Try to have an interesting comment or statement to share—not "just checking." Vary the times of the calls.

"I need to feel *acceptance* regardless of my flaws and mistakes."
1) Focus on the teenager.
    » Love and accept your teen as a person, even when they do things that are unacceptable.
    » Focus on major issues; ignore the minor ones. Ask yourself what you can ignore, including hairstyle, clothing, and condition of the bedroom. Focus on areas that are more important such as attitude, values, and attendance at school and worship.
    » Regularly ask for your teenager's input on what to fix for dinner, what to do over the weekend, or where to go for a Saturday outing. Adopt your teenager's good ideas.
    » Avoid favoritism among siblings. While parents cannot love equally, they can love unconditionally. Find something you like about each child (a character trait, not a physical trait or ability).
    » Do not refer to your teenagers by negative or stereotypical nicknames ("the smart one," "our superstar," "the baby").
    » When your teenager has been rejected by others, be understanding; don't lecture. Say something positive like, "That guy's gonna wake up someday and realize how sorry he is not to have someone with your compassion in his life."
    » Don't compare the performance, ability, or characteristics of one teenager against a sibling, another teenager, or a parent.
2) Forgive and forget your teenager's negative behavior.
    » Let your teenager know that failure is not final.
    » Quickly forgive your teen for something they have done to hurt you, even if they don't ask for forgiveness.

➤ Notice when failure or disappointment happens in your teenager's life, and respond by listening.

"I need to feel *loved* no matter what."

1) Begin with a loving attitude.

➤ Stop thinking about your teenager in critical or negative terms.

➤ Have inside family stories and jokes where a keyword or a signal tips off other family members. Do not make the story or joke about the teenager.

➤ Regularly evaluate your willingness to love your teenager "no strings attached."

➤ Love with God's gracious (undeserved), unconditional (not based on behavior), unlimited (never runs out) love. Be as gracious to your teenager as God is to you when you mess up.

2) Put love into action.

➤ Show affection in physical, appropriate ways—a hug, a back rub, a pat on the back, a wrestling match, or by playing one-on-one basketball.

➤ Always say, "I love you," as your teenager goes out the door for the day, when you drop your teenager off somewhere, at night when your teenager goes out or goes to bed, or at the end of a telephone conversation.

➤ Make eye contact when talking with your teenager.

➤ Find out what love language (see chapter 5) your teenager prefers; then, use that language often.

➤ Develop the habit of daily conversation. It doesn't need to be deep—just regular. Talk where the teenager feels comfortable, not trapped. (For example, talking in the car is easy because both of you are looking forward.)

» When you get angry, speak softly or call time out until you calm down. Don't let conflict escalate into degrading or harmful words or actions.

» Hold hands when you pray at a meal.

» Be spontaneous. Occasionally, show your teenager love by doing something unusual—breakfast in bed, an unbirthday celebration, a surprise trip to a favorite sports event.

» Laugh at yourself, at unexpected events, or at something your teenager thinks is funny—but never at your teenager's actions unless your teenager laughs first.

» Listen without interrupting when your teenager is talking. Don't start thinking about what you need to say to your teenager; just listen.

» Be transparent and vulnerable. Share when you need a hug. (Don't drag out all your problems; just let them know you need love too.)

WHAT TEENAGERS NEED—ARE YOU WILLING TO CHANGE?

As you've read through these actions, what have been your thoughts?

I already do this.

What's so new about these ideas?

No one can do all these things!

These would be perfect things to do in a perfect world, but my teenager will never go for it.

I've already tried these. Nothing works.

Most of us use emotional reasoning—our feelings—to decide what action to take. Emotions can give false information that keeps you stuck where you are. Essentially, you're saying one of the following:

I can't change.

I won't change.

I don't know how to change. (I'm helpless.)

I would change if things were different. (It's hopeless.)

I tried to change, and it didn't work.

Don't ask the wrong question: "Can I change?" Ask the right question: "Will I change?" If what you're doing today isn't working, what happens if you change?

Have you ever stood in your teenager's room at 2 a.m., looking at an empty bed, wondering, *Where could she be at two in the morning? What is she getting into at this time of night?* Are you afraid for his safety? Do you feel guilty for not doing "the right things"? Are you angry at her defiance? Does frustration take over so that you attack your teenager when she finally walks in the door?

• •

YOU CANNOT MAKE YOUR TEENAGER CHANGE. YOU CAN, HOWEVER, CHANGE THE ENVIRONMENT, YOUR ATTITUDE, YOUR ACTIONS, AND YOUR RELATIONSHIP.

• •

What would happen if you hugged your teenager when he got home? How would he feel if you stated that you were glad he was home safely? What would happen if you told your teenager you

202 | **WHY YOUR KIDS DO WHAT THEY DO**

care about him—without attacking his being late? What would happen if you apologized to your teenager for the times your home is a difficult place for your teen to be?

You cannot make your teenager change. You can, however, change the environment, your attitude, your actions, and your relationship. Will you change?

CHAPTER 10

LISTENING TO YOUR TEEN

Teenagers tell me they want to talk to their parents, but their parents are too busy or lack interest. Parents tell me they want to talk to their teenagers, but teenagers never say more than a few words, or they retreat to their bedrooms. Unfortunately, parents tend to talk *at* their teenagers, *through* their teenagers, or *about* their teenagers but never *with* their teenagers. The results look like this.

The 27th annual survey of Who's Who Among American High School Students found these differences in what parents thought and what teenagers did:

Do You Know if Your Teenager Has	Parental Myth	Teenager Reality
contemplated suicide?	9%	26%
cheated?	37%	76%
had sex?	9%	19%
friends with drug problems?	12%	36%
driven drunk?	3%	10%
worried about pregnancy?	22%	44%

These differences occurred among 84 percent of the parents who felt they knew their teenagers well. And these high school juniors and seniors are the leaders in their high schools. Who's Who requires that they have good academic, social, and leadership skills to be chosen. Yet communication with parents was still difficult.

A survey by Partnership for a Drug-Free America found similar results:

Do You Know if Your Teenager Has	Parental Myth	Teenager Reality
tried marijuana?	21%	44%
been offered drugs?	38%	60%
friends who smoke pot?	45%	71%

By now, you know that the motivation behind a teenager's unproductive behavior is an unmet need. But the discrepancy between reality and what a parent believes is happening indicates that help is needed in communicating needs. You won't be able to meet your teenager's needs unless:

1) You know what the need is.
2) You can communicate to your teenager your desire to help.
3) Your teenager responds to your efforts.

IMPROVING COMMUNICATION WITH YOUR TEENAGER

The following are ways you can speak clearly and listen intently so that misunderstandings and conflicts don't undo your best intentions of meeting your teenager's needs.

Six Communication Blockers

Unless you make a determined effort to change, you will talk to your teenagers in the same way your parents talked to you. If you didn't like it then, your teenagers won't like it now. The first steps in improving communication are identifying and avoiding the following communication hindrances.

• •

UNLESS YOU MAKE A DETERMINED EFFORT TO CHANGE, YOU WILL TALK TO YOUR TEENAGERS IN THE SAME WAY YOUR PARENTS TALKED TO YOU. IF YOU DIDN'T LIKE IT THEN, YOUR TEENAGERS WON'T LIKE IT NOW.

• •

1) **The Reporter**—This communication stopper states the facts truthfully but does nothing to encourage their teenager to share the hurt and pain of the moment. Teenagers react to life with their feelings. Their perceptions color reality. Simply stating the facts glosses over their teenager's deeper, more relevant feelings. While statements of logic or fact may be useful in another context, in a conversation with a teenager, facts minus feelings bring conversation to a halt!

2) **The Criticizer**—Criticism is an easy habit to sink into. The job of parenting causes a parent to feel responsible for observing and judging the teen's behavior, then passing on helpful information to promote growth and maturity. This parent may also be prejudiced by other things in the teenager's life, like video games, unusual clothing, or past behavior. An aggressive criticizer may even use derogatory names, put-downs, or teasing. Unfortunately, criticism limits the exchange of feelings.

3) **The Martyr**—This parent plays a game of one-upmanship to turn attention away from the teenager and onto the martyr's personal problem or situation. No matter what the young person faces, the martyr always creates a more personal I'm-worse-off scenario. This communication blocker can be hard to identify because the martyr hides behind the excuse, "I'm just sharing my experiences too. Isn't communication a two-way street?" This argument works with adults. In communicating with a teenager, though, the teenager needs to be the focus.

4) **The Resistor**—This parent blocks communication by refusing to acknowledge the problem. This parent acts indifferently to the teenager's problem, perhaps not responding at all. A variation of this blocker is the parent who leaves a room when the discussion grows heated. These parents fail to connect with their teenagers because they resist the reality in their teenagers' lives.

5) **The Anticipator**—As soon as the teenager starts talking, this parent jumps ahead, defining the problem and identifying the teenager's feelings. This parent anticipates the teenager's thoughts and reactions. This parent interrupts their teenager to express his own thoughts. As a result, this parent doesn't listen at all. Consequently, this teenager doesn't end up talking at all.

6) **The Fixer-Upper**—This parent's intentions are good, but the outcome doesn't help a teenager prepare for life in the real world. As soon as these parents hear pain, frustration, discouragement, or any number of negative emotions, they launch into ways to fix the situation. No project is too small; no cost is too great. Whatever it takes, this parent plows ahead with plans to correct the situation, leaving their teenager wondering what's going on. When a parent moves in to correct the problem without understanding the feelings behind the statements or allowing the teenager to participate in the solution, the parent successfully strips that young person of the ability to figure out his own solutions.

• •

MEETING EMOTIONAL NEEDS INVOLVES SPEAKING IN EMOTIONAL TERMS. THAT INVOLVES A VOCABULARY OF FEELING WORDS.

• •

Stating the facts, expressing criticism, sharing a personal situation, and offering to correct a problem can be useful in some conversations. But these styles of communication block communication between two people who try to connect emotionally. Meeting emotional needs involves speaking in emotional terms. That involves a vocabulary of feeling words. You help your teenagers express their feelings by stating the potential feelings you hear. You also help your teenagers learn to express their feelings by sharing your feelings about their problems. A feeling response encourages further conversation. Listen for the main idea—the main problem—and then make comments like these that open communication further:

"Wow! I can tell you're really angry."

"Sounds like you had a frustrating day."

"It makes me sad to see you so depressed. How can I help?"

"I'd like to hear what happened."

You probably won't even have to ask what happened. Once your teenager hears you express your concern, the explanation can follow. But even if you don't get a further explanation, you have affirmed your interest in your teenager through the language of feeling words.

To avoid being a communication blocker parent, look at the experience from the teenager's point of view. To meet emotional needs, stay in touch with your teenager's emotional world.

While parents see a bigger picture, remember the narrow focus of the world teenagers live in. Looking at the situation from the teenager's perspective enhances your understanding of that young person's feelings.

NINE WAYS TO LISTEN TO TEENAGERS

Most books on parenting teenagers include information about listening as a form of communication. Actually, we are a society of listeners. We listen to podcasts and talk radio in the morning and rush-hour reports in the afternoon. We walk into a room and click on the TV or crank up Spotify to dispel the silence. We listen to reports at work, listen to others on the phone, and listen to talking heads on social media. Even in worship, we listen to music, prayers, meditations, Scripture readings, and sermon clips. Rarely do we listen to the silence. All this listening drowns out what we really need to hear—each other.

Think about the last conversation with your teenager in which you really listened. (Don't count the two sentences you said to your daughter about her homework. Neither can you count your son's asking for money.)

➤➤ What was the main topic of the conversation?
➤➤ Who initiated the conversation?
➤➤ Who did most of the talking? Why?
➤➤ What was the result, outcome, feelings, or expectation from that conversation?
➤➤ How could the conversation have been improved?

Listening is a skill you learn. James 1:19 reminds us that God made us to be listeners first (two ears) and talkers second (one mouth). Eugene Peterson's biblical translation called The Message draws a graphic word picture of this verse—"Lead with your ears, follow up with your tongue, and let anger straggle along in the rear." Somewhere along the way, many parents reverse the order of listening and talking.

In fact, the University of California, Santa Cruz, recently assembled several studies on parent-child communication, finding out that moms and dads communicate differently to their children. Moms are more talkative, use praise, agreement, and approval more often yet tend to be more critical than dads. Dads are more likely to give suggestions, state opinions, and ask more questions.[44] With all that talking, who's listening?

44 Campbell Leaper, Kristin J. Anderson, and Paul Sanders, "Moderator of Gender Effects on Parents' Talk to Their Children: A meta-analysis," Development Psychology 34(1): 3-27 as reported in "Moms and Dads Communicate Differently," Assets Search Institute, Spring 1998, 14.

Below are nine ways you can listen to your teenager. You probably already do some of these. Perhaps one or two will start you thinking of other ways you can improve as a listener.

1) Reflect Back What You Hear

Paraphrase what you hear your teenager say. You can use phrases like, "As I understand, what you're saying is. . . ." "From what you tell me, I gather. . . ." "Listening to what you've said so far. . . ." This indicates that you are listening. WARNING: Using the identical words of the teenager sounds childish and condescending. It comes across as "Psychology 101." No teenager wants to feel like he is being grilled by a shrink. I'll show you what I mean by using a frustrated teenager's statement.

Teenager: "I hate school. Every teacher has it in for me. I can't do anything right. I wish I could quit."

Reflective Parent: "Okay, let me get this straight. Something happened today at school that made you mad."

2) Clarify by Asking Questions

You may have to ask several questions before you get the whole picture. Don't jump to conclusions or offer advice. You've already seen how that stops a conversation. If possible, use the questions to move your teenager to discover their own conclusions. Here's an example:

Teenager: "Yeah, every teacher had it in for me today!"

Clarifying Parent: "What happened? Which teacher are you talking about?"

3) Listen With Your Eyes

Watch your teenager's nonverbal signals. I've heard many times that communication is only 7 percent verbal. The rest is communicated by the speaker's body. Is your teenager's facial expression tense, sad, dark, or glaring? Is their skin color flushed or sallow? Are your teenager's gestures nervous or agitated, like kicking a leg or wringing their hands? Is their posture slumped or erect? Are arms crossed over the chest or flailing in the air? Is breathing shallow and fast or heavy and labored? What tone of voice is involved—angry, sarcastic, silly, gentle? If you will be still and watch, you will hear more than what is spoken.

4) Listen When They Want to Talk

Every parent knows how teenagers tend to pick the worst moments to want to talk. Through some strange phenomenon, a teenager's mouth loosens up more frequently in direct proportion to the lateness of the hour. Whether your daughter comes in late from her out-of-town volleyball game ready to share her experience, or your son stays up late playing video games and then remembers he wants to ask you something, these are the times that parents must be available to talk. The day is coming when you can sleep through the night. Don't miss these valuable moments of reflection and connecting with your teenager. Consider these treasured moments when you tell them through your focused attention how important your teenager is to you.

• •

CONSIDER THESE TREASURED MOMENTS WHEN YOU TELL YOUR TEENAGER THROUGH YOUR FOCUSED ATTENTION HOW IMPORTANT THEY ARE TO YOU.

• •

5) Listen With Courtesy

Treat your teenager with the same respect and kindness you would show to a friend. Do you talk to a friend in loud, angry words? Do you interrupt, jump to conclusions, and offer unsolicited advice? Do you assign blame quickly? Let your demeanor reflect your respect.

Don't hurry when talking with your teenager. When asking questions, allow time for your teenager to form an answer. Most parents don't realize that as mental development occurs in teenagers, communication skills drop. Teenagers frequently search for just the right word. They struggle with translating their thoughts into spoken words. They use the wrong words and get confused easily. I was counseling a young teenager one night when he finally shook his head and said, "I wish my parents could just read my mind!" Give your teenagers space and time to think through what they want to say. Don't try saying it for them unless it's in the reflective, clarifying mode of "Are you saying...?"

6) Listen With Your Touch

As you listen, move closer to your teenager if you think this will encourage your teenager to continue talking. Let your body language show your interest in what is being said. Speak your teenager's name in a positive manner as you engage with them in conversation. If appropriate, place your hand on your teenager's arm or shoulder. Acknowledge their feelings with simple words or phrases like "Oh," "I see," "Wow!" or "Hmm." Sometimes your words aren't even important.

A mom recently told me how she walked into her kitchen late one afternoon to start dinner and found her twelve-year-old daughter crying at the kitchen counter. Without saying a word, the mother gathered her daughter in her arms and held her until the weeping stopped. She offered her daughter a tissue as the girl headed toward her bedroom. The mother never learned the reason for the emotions her daughter was expressing through her tears.

7) Listen With Wisdom and Innocence

As parents, you should strive to "be as shrewd as snakes and as innocent as doves" (Matthew 10:16) as you communicate with your teenage children. Be wise about the world of teenagers. Know the temptations they face every day. Stay in touch with your teenager's world. Don't assume that "It's not happening to my kid!" At the same time, don't assume the worst of your teenager without a pattern of behavior. Be innocent as you listen and learn. If you keep an open mind and don't jump to conclusions, you have a better chance of understanding your teenager and seeing and feeling things from their perspective.

8) Listen by Example

Communicate in the same manner that you want your teenager to talk with you. Speak in an honoring, pleasant voice. When you get angry, avoid sarcasm and red-flag words—those that create additional feelings of anger, name-calling, or useless threats. Listen when the other person talks. Be comfortable with the fact that you and your teenager can disagree and still talk to one another. Above all, live your life consistently with what you preach. Teenagers may not hear all you say, but they watch everything you do.

9) Listen With Courage

Talking with a teenager is tough. You never know where a conversation will lead. You want to know what's going on in his life, but you hesitate to learn the truth. Listening takes courage. Listening without having the final word means you are letting your teenager grow up. Listening without offering advice means you are letting your teenager learn how to make decisions on their own.

• •

THINK ABOUT ALL THE DON'TS TEENAGERS HEAR IN THEIR WORLD. IF YOUR TEENAGER ASKS FOR SOMETHING, BE COURAGEOUS, AND SEE IF THERE'S ANY WAY YOU CAN SAY YES. WEIGH THE POSITIVE RESPONSE WITH THE POSSIBILITY OF BUILDING TRUST AND MATURITY.

• •

One way to be courageous is to say yes as much as possible. Think about all the *don'ts* teenagers hear in their world. If your teenager asks for something, be courageous, and see if there's any way you can say yes. Weigh the positive response with the possibility of building trust and maturity.

Listening can be painful, joyful, enlightening, confusing, discouraging, fun, adventuresome, hopeless, and hopeful. As you listen, you may experience the same range of emotions that your teenager feels. But if you remain determined to meet your teenager conversationally, one day, you may hear, "Thanks for being there when I needed to talk. I could always count on you."

A FIVE-STEP PROCESS TO REDUCE AND RESOLVE CONFLICT

No matter how effectively you communicate, conflict happens between parents and teenagers. The best way to handle conflict is to consider your options before you get into the heat of battle.

This five-step framework for dealing with conflict offers you several practical ideas for defusing, reducing, or eliminating the conflict before it escalates into World War III. Keep in mind that you are not trying to end up with winners and losers but with good, healthy relationships and respect.

• •

TAKE A "TIME-OUT" IF THE CONFLICT GETS HEATED. BUT, DO NOT WALK AWAY WITHOUT AN EXPLANATION AND A TIME TO CONTINUE. ("WE'RE GETTING TOO ANGRY. LET'S TAKE TEN MINUTES TO COOL DOWN AND THEN TRY AGAIN.")

• •

Step 1: Confront the Problem Quickly

Conflict can begin over just about anything—misunderstandings, hurt feelings, lack of attention, unfair treatment, false accusations, or even a casual conversation that develops into an argument. Perhaps you hurt your teenager by being abrupt or self-absorbed. Your teenager may have hurt you with unkind words. If left unresolved, bitterness, broken trust, fear, guilt, and anger can damage the relationship. As soon as you realize there is a problem, talk about it.

- ‣ Go directly to your teenager. Don't talk to others in your family while avoiding the person involved. Although you may talk with your spouse about the problem, don't expect your spouse or another child to get involved if the conflict is between you and your teenager. ("Triangles" in relationships cause problems.)
- ‣ Attack the problem or the hurtful action, not your teenager. ("I love you, but I don't like your tone of voice or your words.")
- ‣ Take a "time-out" if the conflict gets heated. You won't solve the problem when both people are too angry to think rationally. But, do NOT walk away without an explanation and a time to continue. ("We're getting too angry. Let's take ten minutes to cool down and then try again.")
- ‣ Several counselors use a system called the speaker and the listener. Psychologists and brothers Greg and Michael Smalley explain this process. "The speaker's job is to express feelings and needs. . . . It's important for the speaker to keep his wording short and not make long, drawn-out statements. The listener's job is to pay close attention and

repeat exactly what he hears the speaker express."[45] After the speaker feels they have been heard, then the roles are reversed. The Smalleys remind us that you are not working to gain agreement but to help both sides feel that they've been heard and understood.

Step 2: Maintain Your Self-Control

John Drakeford and Claude King, in their book for lay counseling, *Wise Counsel*, explain the importance of remembering that you are the adult in the relationship and need to stay in control:

Much talk by the teenager will sound unreasonable if not downright impertinent. Make allowances for the brashness of immature youth. If he loses his temper, do not descend to his level by losing yours.[46]

»» Don't take the bait. Teenagers are notorious for knowing how to push our hot buttons. They can say something ("You're mean; you don't really care about me!") that we feel needs defending ("I do care. That's ridiculous."), and the argument begins. You took the bait. Instead, learn to say in a calm voice, "I'm not going to fight with you."

»» Use "I" messages rather than the accusatory "you" messages. Your teenager immediately turns defensive when the sentence begins with, "You did. . . ." Or, "You should have. . . ." An "I" message starts with your feelings or how you are affected—"I am hurt. . . ." Or, "I'm concerned about. . . ."

45 Greg Smalley and Michael Smalley, "Got Conflict with Teens? Communicate!" *Living with Teenagers*, April 1997, 21.

46 John Drakeford and Claude King, *Wise Counsel* (Nashville, TN: LifeWay Press, 1993), 167.

>> Own up to your failures. Be willing to say if you've made a mistake. Ask for forgiveness.

Step 3: Show Concern Through Your Response and Reaction

Reduce the tension and conflict by speaking in a calm voice with gentle, carefully thought-out words. Use the listening skills I mentioned earlier in this chapter. Maintain eye contact with your teenager, so they can see your concern and willingness to listen.

Step 4: Work on a Compromise

As you and your teenager try to resolve the conflict, consider these ideas.

>> Make a list of all the possibilities or options without judging or criticizing any comment until the list is complete.

>> Eliminate those ideas that aren't practical or safe. Decide on the options to consider.

>> If you get stuck trying to think of options, start a new thought line by asking, "Have you thought about. . . ?" or "What would happen if you. . . ?"

>> If you have reached a stalemate and can't come up with a solution, you may need a third party. Choose someone who is acceptable and respected by you and your teenager—an uninvolved, unbiased person like another parent, a youth minister, or a family counselor who can hear both sides and help you reach a compromise.

>> Realize that there are some areas where there can be no compromise. For example, it should never be acceptable

for a teenager to talk about hurting someone, taking illegal drugs, or breaking the law in any way.

Step 5: Cultivate the Relationship

Even after conflict has occurred, be quick to forgive your teenager or to ask for your teenager's forgiveness, so you can maintain the relationship. If the conflict is not completely handled, continue to talk about the problem until it no longer bothers either of you. Don't let anything become a barrier between you and your teenager. You'll have enough of those to overcome during your teenager's growing-up years.

WHAT TO DO WHEN TEENAGERS WON'T TALK

Don't panic! It's actually normal. As teenagers gain their independence, they tend to turn to their friends for conversation and advice. Even when teenagers know their parents want to talk and are willing to listen, talking to their parents feels like they are giving up hard-earned freedom and space. You are not alone. A lack of communication with teenagers happens in all families.

If your normally chatty teenager suddenly becomes sullen or secretive or withdrawn, look for other possibilities. Look past the silent surface to find the real culprit. Stress at school, in a sport, or with friends creates an emotionally drained teenager who may be worn out. A teenager may feel guilty or ashamed. Perhaps your teenager has been angry or hurt. A teenager may fear rejection or judgment or punishment without having a chance to offer a fair explanation. Some teenagers don't want a parent's advice, so they never mention the problem. Some teenagers are so laid back that they haven't learned how to actually talk with others.

• •

BOTH PARENTS AND TEENAGERS CAN DEVELOP SELECTIVE HEARING, CHOOSING TO RESPOND TO ONLY WHAT THEY WANT TO HEAR.

• •

Both parents and teenagers can develop selective hearing, choosing to respond to only what they want to hear. Poor communication skills keep younger teenagers from expressing their feelings. Some young people think their parents don't care, are too busy, don't know what's going on in the real world, or don't know how to help. Teenagers will stop talking if a parent betrays their trust. I've had many teenagers complain that their parents repeated their secrets to friends and neighbors.

The following ideas may increase your chances of conversation with your teenager; however, there are no guarantees. Pick and choose what might work for you. If it doesn't work, try another approach.

Create a Listening Environment

Commit to a time for daily conversation. Dinner offers a great time to talk about events. Unfortunately, about 20 percent of today's teenagers never eat a meal with their parents.[47] Opening doors in your home, showing a willingness to turn off the phones or turn down (or off) the TV, and sharing specific activities with individual teenagers all create opportunities for the teenager to talk.

---

47 Carolyn Kitch, "How to Talk So Your Teen-Ager Will Listen," *Reader's Digest*, May 1997, 107.

Try "Parallel Conversation"

Although most communication experts say to look a person in the eyes when you talk with them, teenagers are different. Sometimes they are more likely to talk when you aren't looking at each other as you do something else. For example, talk during a car ride where both you and your teenager are watching the road. Parallel conversation can also happen while working in the yard, shooting baskets, taking a walk around the neighborhood, or even watching TV together. In parallel conversation, the emphasis is on the activity; the talking is incidental.

Ask for Your Teenager's Advice

Let your teenager help you think through a problem. ("I have to give a speech tomorrow on the number one problem in America today. What do you think that is?" "How can I get my third-graders interested in math? You like math; what would you do?") If your teenager asks you about one of their problems, don't offer advice too quickly. After gathering the facts, ask your teenager what they want to see happen. Encourage them to weigh the pros and cons.

Use Other Forms of Communication

A young friend of mine says, "Talking makes my ears tired." I agree. Sometimes, we don't hear because we can't listen anymore. Communicate in other ways. Written messages give a formal importance to the information. Sticky notes make it possible to leave brief messages in wonderfully creative places to surprise and encourage your teenager. Send a text message or voice note of admiration to your teen. Write a letter of support to your teenager before a difficult event or during a major decision. Some parents won't talk to their teenagers about issues like sex, but you can write a note stating your values and standards in a straightforward way. If you need a response from them, make out a checklist or other brief ways for them to reply back to you.

Send a video message from your phone with an affirming message on crucial days like the day of a big test, competition, or the final game of the season. Ask a question at the end of the video that encourages your teenager to continue the conversation with you later.

Wish along with your teenager. Your teenager knows when you can and can't grant a fantasy, but saying things like "I wish I could make it go away," "I wish you could live today over again too," "I wish we had the money to get a better car," or, "Wouldn't it be fun to take off for the beach today?!" Let your teenager know you understand those feelings of longing.

Ask effective questions to get responses.

AVOID the following: "How was your day?" "What did you do today?" "How's it going?" These don't require much comment from your teenager.

ASK: If you really want to know, build off an event that was supposed to happen that day. Your teenager may be surprised you remembered. "How do you feel about your quiz? How did the other students feel like they did?"

AVOID any question that can be answered with a "yes," "no," or a grunt! Teenagers are notorious for responses like "I dunno," "It's not my problem," or "Yeah."

ASK questions that are open-ended, that call for an opinion or feeling, or that uncover new information. Open-ended questions allow your teenager to express both thoughts and feelings. Questions might be:

"What led up to that?"

"What did you do then?"

"How do you feel about the situation?"

AVOID "Why?" questions that put the other person on the defensive. "Why did you do that?" These types of questions sound like you doubt your teenager.

ASK: "What?" and "How?" These questions tend to provoke more of a response. Combine these with encouraging phrases like "Go on...." or "I'd like to know what happened."

Take what you can get. Talkative teenagers who become non-responsive may want a little more independence. If you work to keep those communication lines up and flowing most of the time, these teenagers will return to talk to you another day.

• •

TAKE WHAT YOU CAN GET. IF YOUR TALKATIVE TEENAGER BECOMES LESS TALKATIVE, STILL KEEP THE COMMUNICATION LINES UP AND FLOWING. YOUR TEEN WILL RETURN TO TALK TO YOU ANOTHER DAY.

• •

"WHEN I SAY . . . , I NEED. . . ."

Practice listening to your teenager with an awareness of his or her needs. Occasionally, a teenager may say, "I need a hug!" but most of the time, the message is more oblique. Use these commonly spoken phrases to determine what your teenager might need. There are no right or wrong answers. You can also write down phrases you've heard your teenager say recently and decide which need is involved.

The Noticed Gauge	The Encour-agement Gauge	The Empathy Gauge	The Direction Gage	The Security Gauge
attention	nurtured	comfort	significance	security
respect	supported		purpose	acceptance
valued				loved

_____ 1) "You don't care what happens to me."
_____ 2) "My head hurts."
_____ 3) "Did you notice that I put gas in the car yesterday?"
_____ 4) "Is anyone going to be at my game tonight?"
_____ 5) "Doesn't anyone knock around here?"
_____ 6) "This is too hard."
_____ 7) "I forgot to mow the lawn; sorry."
_____ 8) "Nobody's going on that boring retreat; why do I have to go?"
_____ 9) "I mess up every time I try."
_____ 10) "I can't wait to get out of here for good!"
_____ 11) "I didn't get the job."
_____ 12) "Nobody showed up but me."
_____ 13) "I can't be your perfect child!"
_____ 14) "What were you and mom fighting about last night?"
_____ 15) "I hate my hair."
_____ 16) "Don't expect me to bring home all A's."
_____ 17) "Why doesn't someone ask me what I'd like to do?"

_____ 18) "I don't care what happens to her; she's not my problem."

_____ 19) "No one will miss me if I don't go."

_____ 20) "You always let Pat go. Why can't I?"

Jean and Karl worried about their fourteen-year-old son, Kevin. About six months earlier, he had suddenly become secretive, hiding behind his closed bedroom door and avoiding all contact with the family. Determined to keep Kevin in touch with the family even if he were going through his teenage years, Jean and Karl made Kevin join them and their other two children for a day at a local amusement park.

At first, Kevin moped around, but within an hour of arriving at the park, he was laughing and screaming and acting like the old Kevin. That night after a full day of fun, Kevin's parents knocked on his bedroom door to thank him for going with them. During the conversation, Karl asked, "Is something wrong? Your mom and I have been worried about you for several months, but today proves you still love being with us as a family. We want you to know we love you. Please, let us know how we can help."

Quickly, Kevin told them what challenges he had been going through. Several older kids at school had offered Kevin marijuana. He didn't know what to do, so he'd been smoking it with them after school. He felt trapped—and guilty. The only way he knew to handle it was to withdraw. Fortunately, Jean and Karl didn't blow up. Instead, they sat down and calmly talked with Kevin about what he was doing. They talked through his situation and laid out his next steps to stop doing what he was doing and how he could distance himself from these friends.

Later, Karl told me how shocked they were upon hearing what their son was doing, but he was determined to help Kevin grow stronger through the situation and the choices he was making. His efforts paid off in open communication before Kevin continued down the wrong path.

CHAPTER 11

HEALING
THE HURTS

Recently, after a speaking engagement, I was walking out to the church parking lot with the associate pastor and his wife. Before we went our separate ways, the pastor asked me to keep his eighteen-year-old son in my prayers. I asked if there was anything specific I could pray for. As the pastor and his wife looked at each other, they both began to tear up. For about the next twenty minutes, they shared the hurt and anguish their son had brought to their family. Their son was currently living at home but waiting for his trial date to determine how severe his punishment was going to be. He had been arrested for making and selling an illegal drug. This was his second arrest, and it looked like he was going to face three to five years of prison time.

The pastor shared with me how his former church had asked him to resign because of the troubles with their son. As you can imagine, this couple was living with an enormous amount of

227

humiliation and embarrassment, as well as rejection from those they had considered to be their closest friends. Even though they had sought help from a professional counselor, the hurt was still there. Fortunately, their new church where they were serving was very supportive and encouraging to this hurting family.

The pastor asked me if I would be willing to talk with his son. I told him I would be happy to, so I arranged to take his son out for lunch the next day. Knowing there was little I could do, I tried to assure the young man that his parents loved him very much and only wanted the best for him. As we talked, he shared with me how he was coping with the embarrassment and pain in his own life. He knew he had hurt his family greatly and was very remorseful. I challenged him to reconcile with his family, especially his parents. He assured me that he would.

Early Tuesday morning, as the associate pastor took me back to the airport, he told me that their family had stayed up until 2:00 a.m. that morning, working through a lot of issues that had hurt their family relationships. He told me that even though his son was still going to suffer the consequences of his crime, as a family, he felt they were finally at peace with their son.

• •

**WHILE EFFECTIVE COMMUNICATION
CAN CREATE AND RESTORE SOME
PARENT-TEEN RELATIONSHIPS, FOR
MANY FAMILIES, THIS IS NOT ENOUGH.**

• •

While effective communication can create and restore some parent-teen relationships, for many families, this is not enough. Their wounds are too deep. Their hurt is too intense. For them, the pain continues no matter what they say or do. To meet the needs of their teenagers, these families must handle past wounds, identify the problems that caused the pain, grieve for the broken relationships, and move toward forgiveness. Easy to say—tough to do!

IDENTIFY THE WOUNDS: HURT BROUGHT ON BY THE TEENAGER

The list of damaging behaviors that teenagers pursue can be extensive and still not include the action or behavior that paralyzes your family. It is necessary, however, to identify the situation that causes the hurt before healing can begin. From the list below, select the behavior(s) that you feel has caused the hurt that needs healing in your family. Write in other behaviors that relate to your family's current emotional status.

❏ use of drugs	❏ sexual activity and/or alcohol	❏ school dropout
❏ uncontrolled rage	❏ eating disorders	❏ pregnancy
❏ trouble with the law	❏ verbal abuse	❏ smoking
❏ self-mutilation	❏ reckless driving	❏ pornography
❏ attempted suicide	❏ homosexuality	❏ runaway

Although some activities happened in the past, they still can control family relationships. And teenagers are not the only ones who create hard-to-heal wounds. Parents bear responsibility too.

IDENTIFY THE WOUNDS: HURT BROUGHT ON BY THE PARENTS

In several of these situations, you may feel more like the victim and less like the one causing the pain. Yet it is important to understand how these situations and behaviors can hold family relationships hostage. Several areas will be defined, so you can see what's involved and how a parent fits into the situation. As you read through these actions, be honest with yourself rather than taking a defensive position. Admitting the problem is the first vital step to healing.

Marital Difficulties, Divorce, Remarriage

- ❏ Marital conflict, but still living together
- ❏ Marital conflict resulting in separation
- ❏ Marital conflict resulting in divorce
- ❏ Remarriage with no other children involved except the teenager
- ❏ Remarriage with no other children involved

Disruptive Family Patterns

Disruptive family patterns continue to be a major cause of a teenager's wounds:

- ➤ Only 18 percent of American households are families with married parents.[48]
- ➤ Approximately 40-50 of first marriages end in divorce. The divorce rate for second marriages is even higher, with

---

48 US Census Bureau, "Census Bureau Releases New Estimates on America's Families and Living Arrangements," *Census.gov*, 30 Nov. 2021, https://www.census.gov/newsroom/press-releases/2021/families-and-living-arrangements.html.

approximately 60-67 percent of second marriages ending in divorce.[49]

» Twenty-four million children live in single-family households.[50]

» Nearly 80 percent of single-parent households are headed by single mothers.[51]

» About one-third of the single-parent households in which the mother is the sole provider live in poverty.[52] That is almost four times the number of two-parent households.[53]

» A total of about 13 million—1 in 4 children under the age of 18—are being raised without a father.[54]

Divorce

In an extensive study of the effects of divorce on children conducted by Judith Wallerstein, sixty families were observed over a twenty-five-year period. Each family was chosen because the parents were in the process of divorcing. Through her study, Wallerstein learned how divorce affects children:

49 Petrelli Previtera, "Divorce Statistics for 2022." *Petrelli Previtera, LLC,* 9 Jan. 2023, https://www.petrellilaw.com/divorce-statistics-for-2022/#:~:text=What%20Percent%20of%20Marriages%20End,second%20marriages%20ending%20in%20divorce.

50 The Annie E. Casey Foundation, "Child Well-Being in Single-Parent Families," *The Annie E. Casey Foundation,* 1 Aug. 2022, https://www.aecf.org/blog/child-well-being-in-single-parent-families?gclid=CjOKCQjw8qmhBhClARIsANAtbocdOKvEN8r9QKz5JBIJQQ-mvMnk6FuOZIR1-_uDiDRSmA4col6R80oaAjSXEALw_wcB.

51 US Census Bureau, "Census Bureau Releases New Estimates on America's Families and Living Arrangements," *Census.gov,* 17 Nov. 2022, https://www.census.gov/newsroom/press-releases/2022/americas-families-and-living-arrangements.html.

52 "Single Mother Statistics (Updated 2023)," *SMG,* 2 Feb. 2023, https://singlemotherguide.com/single-mother-statistics/.

53 National Center for Juvenile Justice, *Poverty Status of Children by Family Structure, 2020,* https://www.ojjdp.gov/ojstatbb/population/qa01203.asp?qaDate=2020.

54 Jack Brewer. "Fatherlessness and Its Effects on American Society." *AFPI,* 15 Feb. 2022, https://americafirstpolicy.com/latest/20220215-fatherlessness-and-its-effects-on-american-society#:~:text=Across%20America%2C%20there%20are%20approximately,children%20(Father%20Absence%20Statistics).

» One-third of the children never pursued any schooling beyond high school.

» Before the age of fourteen, 50 percent of the children participated in serious substance abuse, with only two families intervening and getting help for their children.

» Although many of the fathers were professionals, none of them provided full financial support for the teenager through college; one-fourth of the dads refused to provide financial aid; one-third of the dads offered partial support.

» Many of the young people, particularly the girls, became sexually active early.

» Only 25 percent of the children married, and two later divorced.[55]

The divorces in this study occurred when the children were between two and six years old, yet the destructive behavior surfaced during adolescence. Wallerstein observed:

Unlike the adult experience, the child's suffering does not reach its peak at the breakup and then level off. On the contrary. Divorce is a cumulative experience for the child. It's [sic] impact increases over time.[56]

Abuse
❏ physical abuse
❏ emotional abuse
❏ sexual abuse

---

55 Peter Wendel, "Counseling children of divorce," *Counseling Today* Online, September 1997,

www.counseling.org/ctonline/archives/CT099 7/ct099 7a10.htm and Elizabeth Fernandez, "Grim legacy of divorce," *The Atlanta Journal- Constitution* June 3, 1997, F5.

56 Fernandez, "Grim legacy of divorce."

According to Josh McDowell, a child abuse case is reported every ten seconds in the United States.[57] McDowell defines physical abuse as "all acts that create injury or a substantial and unnecessary risk of injury. Violent shaking or slapping, shoving, kicking, and punching are all forms of physical abuse."[58] Emotional abuse is more difficult to determine because it involves verbal attacks, blaming, or belittling, but it also may include an attitude of disrespect for the teenager. Other than the noticeable signs of abuse, such as bruises or burns, a teenager may experience these problems: guilt, lack of trust, aggression, poor social skills, emotional withdrawal, or a tendency to run away.

Sexual abuse involves any kind of sexual contact, observation, or conversation between someone and a child with the exploiter receiving sexual gratification from the experience. The exploiter can be someone in the family (including another child) or someone outside the family. McDowell identifies these results of sexual abuse: physical and medical problems, pregnancy, guilt, shame, feelings of helplessness, low self-esteem, repeating the abusive behavior on another person, and generally poor social and relational skills.[59]

Other Hurts
❏ rage or uncontrolled anger
❏ neglect (defined as a parent's failure to take care of the child's basic needs and well-being in an adequate way)
❏ long-term illness

---

57 Josh McDowell, *Josh McDowell's Handbook on Counseling Youth* (Waco, TX: Word Publishing, 1996), 359.
58 McDowell, *Josh McDowell's Handbook on Counseling Youth.*
59 McDowell, *Josh McDowell's Handbook on Counseling Youth,* 350-351.

❏ change in job (fired, "phased out," or demoted; new location involving a move; promotion involving more time away from family)

❏ death of family member that you are still grieving

❏ substance abuse (alcohol and/or drugs)

❏ other

Define the hurt in your family and how your family feels about this situation.

➤ The event that has created the greatest hurt in our family is
    _____.

➤ The way I feel about this is _____
    _____.

➤ The way my teenager feels about this is _____
    _____.

➤ The way other family members feel about this is _____
    _____.

➤ What do you think must happen for this hurt to heal? _____
    _____.

IDENTIFY GRIEF, GUILT, AND OTHER FEELINGS

Being wounded can result in emotions and feelings that prevent the hurt from healing. Here are just a few of the emotions you or other family members may have experienced.

➤ Pride: "What will other people think?" "This makes me look like I'm a lousy parent."

➤ Guilt: "Where did I go wrong?" "It must be my fault."

» Anger: "How could he do that to me?" "I can't believe she expected us to stand by and do nothing."

» Shame: "I can never show my face in public again." "Everyone's going to know what happened."

» Loneliness: "I can't talk to anyone; it's just too personal."

» Fear: "Will we ever be a normal family again?" "Do her poor choices place us all in jeopardy?"

» Grief: "I've lost the most precious part of me." "He's breaking my heart."

» Bitterness: "This was intentional. He meant to hurt me." "She always does something to make me feel lousy."

This is not a definitive list of emotions. Perhaps you have experienced other feelings. Are you surprised that some emotions keep returning, even when you've tried to suppress them? Daniel Goleman, author of the best-seller *Emotional Intelligence*, explains how emotions continually reappear without warning:

When some feature of an event seems similar to an emotionally charged memory from the past, the emotional mind responds by triggering the feeling that went with the remembered event. The emotional mind reacts to the present as though it were the past. . . . Thoughts and reactions at this moment will take on the coloration of thoughts and reactions then, even though it may seem that the reaction is due solely to the circumstance of the moment. Our emotional mind will harness the rational mind to its purpose, so we come up with explanations for our feelings and reactions— rationalizations—justifying them in terms of the present moment, without realizing the influence of the emotional memory.[60]

60 Daniel Goleman, *Emotional Intelligence* (New York, NY: Bantam Books, 1995), 295-96.

So while you think you've dealt with an emotion, every time a similar situation occurs, the emotion pops up. Glossing over your feelings doesn't deal with the problem or the resulting emotions.

One of the strongest emotions associated with a past hurt is guilt. Whether you did the wounding or you were the one wounded by another's behavior, guilt appears. If, for example, you and your spouse divorced, perhaps you feel guilty for the damage done to your children. If your teenager is participating in a dangerous activity that you know is wrong, you may feel guilty for not meeting that teenager's need.

Sometimes the guilt can be overwhelming, leaving you paralyzed and frustrated. Other times the guilt is more painful than the hurt. Actually, the pain of guilt can be a warning sign that protects relationships. For example, if a person feels guilty for a certain behavior, the pain from the guilt may stop the person from continuing the behavior. Bruce Hamstra explains the difference between good guilt and bad guilt:

➤ Good guilt serves as a compass for your personal standards.
➤ Good guilt helps you to control destructive, hurtful impulses.
➤ Good guilt allows you to experience the pain of your mistakes and take corrective actions.
➤ Good guilt, if honestly acknowledged, can lead to personal growth, the making of amends, and perhaps even forgiveness.
➤ Guilt is not helpful when it stems from things that are truly not your fault.
➤ Guilt is not helpful when you have unintentionally hurt or neglected someone, although apologies may be in order.

➤ Guilt is not helpful when it's unfairly used by others to manipulate you or impede your personal growth.

➤ Guilt is not helpful when the hurtful acts were not foreseeable or preventable.

➤ Guilt is not helpful when your thoughts, feelings, or actions didn't actually hurt anyone else.[61]

Look over Hamstra's list. Circle the type of guilt you feel. This may take more thought than a cursory reading. Figure out what kind of guilt you have and what has caused the feeling. Here's an example: Your family is hurting because you must spend time, energy, and effort taking care of an elderly parent. You may feel guilty for not spending time with your teenager. Hamstra points out that "bad guilt" is not helpful when the illness is not your fault.

• •

YOU SAW THE IMPORTANCE OF GRIEVING THE LOSS OF UNMET NEEDS IN YOUR LIFE. GRIEVING THE HURT IN FAMILY RELATIONSHIPS BRINGS HEALING TOO.

• •

You saw the importance of grieving the loss of unmet needs in your life. Grieving the hurt in family relationships brings healing too. You may have already shed many tears over the painful situation that has wounded your family. It may not be necessary to cry

---

61 Bruce Hamstra, *Why Good People Do Bad Things* (New York, NY: Carol Publishing Group, 1996), 37-38.

again, but it is necessary to realize that, in some way, the family has been hurt, damaged, or experienced a broken relationship. In divorce, the grief is often not recognized because of the feelings of failure. But divorce is the end of a relationship, and that deserves to be grieved. You may have to grieve the fact that your teenager is not living up to your hopes and expectations. You may have to grieve that your teenager has made poor choices and now must suffer the consequences. You may have to grieve that you have hurt others with your poor choices. For some, grief is a private matter. For others, it helps to grieve and receive comfort. Don't bypass this important step in healing.

→→ For what do you need to grieve?
→→ With whom can you share this grief?

FIND FORGIVENESS AND REPENTANCE

Are you content to live with the guilt and pain in your family, or do you want to move on? To deal with the wounding, you can blame others, society, your teenager, the circumstances, or even God, or you can seek forgiveness. If you are the one who has been wounded, then you can do the forgiving. If you are the one who has created the hurtful situation, then you must ask for forgiveness.

Hamstra explains the great value of forgiveness:

Forgiveness is a powerful equalizer: It helps free the victim of the bitterness and anger that eats away at the spirit while at the same time liberating the perpetrator from much of his or her guilt. It allows all involved a better chance to get on with their lives.[62]

---

62 Hamstra, *Why Good People Do Bad Things*, 46.

If you have been the one who has hurt the family, your asking for forgiveness starts the healing process. Asking for forgiveness is more than saying, "I'm sorry." This shallow approach is dispensed too often without sincerity. A sincere request for forgiveness might sound like this: "I was wrong. I made mistakes that hurt you. I regret my part in hurting you. I want to change the feelings between us."

This turns forgiveness into repentance. Repentance involves both a change of mind (a new attitude) and a change of direction (a different action). We are most familiar with asking God for forgiveness. And God is the place to start as you work to restore a relationship within your family. Be direct in stating the hurtful action that needs forgiveness. State your repentance by asking God to begin the healing. Next, go to those in your family, including your teenager, who has been affected by your wounding action. Confess your hurtful action honestly. You might say something like the statements above or like this: "I'm trying to rebuild our relationship. I am hurting because I have hurt you. I want things to be better between us. Please forgive me for my hurtful action. I can make excuses, but they don't really matter. I just want things to be better between us."

Is an apology enough? I don't think so. Here's the hard part. You must live your repentance before the other person. Show your changed attitude by relating to your teenager in a caring, concerned way. Don't repeat the offending behavior. Draw strength from knowing God has already forgiven you.

Thinking about your own situation:

» Ask God's forgiveness: _____
_____.

» Write out an apology to your teenager and other family members if they were involved _____
_____.

» List several ways you can live your repentance before your family _____
_____
_____.

If you have been the one who was wounded by your teenager's behavior, you can offer forgiveness. David Augsburger, in *The Freedom of Forgiveness*, suggests a four-step process of forgiveness.

» *Forgive immediately* before bitterness, guilt, or hurt get into your thoughts and turn into vindictive revenge. Augsburger suggests the way to handle bitterness once it has taken hold is to "stop thinking about yourself. Don't tolerate those thoughts of self-pity. Don't permit those angry thoughts of self-defensiveness to master you."[63] To heal, you must stop the cycle of hurt and get on with life.

» *Forgive continually* so that you are focused on others, rather than yourself. This way of life means that you accept others. This is not a shallow tolerance of others or letting others manipulate your feelings. Forgiveness does not condone the action. It does not depend on any change in the offender's

---

63 David Augsburger, *The Freedom of Forgiveness* (Chicago, IL: Moody Press, 1970), 35.

behavior. There are no guarantees that the offensive behavior won't happen again. Continual forgiveness, however, realizes that life is too valuable to spend in anger, self-pity, or revenge. You will only have this teenager in your home for a few short years, then the teenager goes off into the world. Even in close families, children form lives of their own, and parents learn to live in "an empty nest." Forgive, so these last few years together can be pleasant, anticipated times, rather than bitter, sad, difficult days.

➤➤ *Forgive and forget.* It may not be possible to completely remove the hurt from your memory or the consequences of the hurt from reality. It is possible, however, to stop rehashing the problem with "if onlys" and "what ifs." When you forgive and forget, the situation no longer has power over you. You have chosen to let those old feelings go. Forgiveness is for the forgiver's protection and peace of mind.

➤➤ *Forgive and be healed.* Forgiveness is an active word. You can express your forgiveness before the teenager asks for forgiveness. You might say, "I forgive you for hurting me by your habitual drinking. I don't like your behavior and I'm going to help you stop. But I love you, and I'm not going to let this come between us." This kind of forgiveness brings healing, according to Augsburger:

[It is] acceptance with no exception. It accepts not only the hurt you've received, but it accepts the one who did the hurting, and it accepts the loss caused by the hurtful actions or words. It makes no exceptions.[64]

64 Augsburger, *The Freedom of Forgiveness*, 39-40.

You can forgive, forget, and be healed because Christ did it for you.

WHEN TO ASK FOR HELP

Asking for professional help is not a sign of weakness but of strength. You are saying, "I am doing the best job I can, but God has not gifted me in understanding all I need to know in order to help my teenager (or in order to help myself). So I need help." A professional counselor can determine the extent to which your teenager needs professional help and, more importantly, can give both you and your teenager perspective on the situation. Before seeking professional help, use these questions suggested by psychotherapist and psychologist Les Parrott to determine whether to involve a counselor or not. Remember also that you need to be concerned about a pattern of behavior, not necessarily a single incident.[65]

- ▸▸ Is your teenager quiet for long periods of time or withdrawn from friends and regular activities?
- ▸▸ Is your teenager close to dropping out of or failing school?
- ▸▸ Is your teenager obsessed with food, diets, and exercise?
- ▸▸ Is your teenager involved in any form of self-mutilation (cuts, burns, teeth marks)?
- ▸▸ Does your teenager fear being left alone with a member of your family, a neighbor, or some other person? Is there any chance sexual abuse has occurred or is taking place now?
- ▸▸ Is your teenager depressed?
- ▸▸ Is your teenager interested in the occult or black magic?

---

65 Parrott, *Helping the Struggling Adolescent*, 41-42.

➤ Is your teenager involved in numerous situations of vandalism or fights?

➤ Is your teenager sexually active?

• •

ASKING FOR PROFESSIONAL HELP IS NOT A SIGN OF WEAKNESS BUT OF STRENGTH. YOU ARE SAYING, "I AM DOING THE BEST JOB I CAN, BUT GOD HAS NOT GIFTED ME IN UNDERSTANDING ALL I NEED TO KNOW IN ORDER TO HELP MY TEENAGER (OR IN ORDER TO HELP MYSELF). SO I NEED HELP."

• •

➤ Is your teenager hearing voices, hallucinating, or out of touch with reality?

➤ Is your teenager having morbid thoughts or talking about death?

➤ Is your teenager having trouble sleeping, eating, or staying focused on a task, or is there any other radical change in behavior?

➤ Is your teenager drinking, driving and drinking, using drugs, or huffing paint, glue, or other substance?

➤ Is your teenager experiencing panic attacks with intense periods of anxiety?

To find professional help, ask your family physician, a minister, a school counselor, or friends with teenagers for referrals. I would like to make a strong suggestion concerning a counselor you choose. If at all possible, find a good Christian counselor. You need someone who can help you and your family deal with the difficult issues you may be facing from a Christ-centered approach. A preliminary phone call to the professional will give you information about that person's areas of specialization and expectations. Another possibility is to join a support group for either you or your teenager. There are many secular support groups available; however, be sure to check with your local church first to see what support groups they offer before you jump into a secular program.

LOOK TOWARD RECOVERY

Once forgiveness is offered, healing can begin. You may not feel like everything is back to normal (whatever that is when living with a teenager!), but you should see improvement in your relationship with your teenager. And you should be able to implement the process of meeting needs more effectively. The following ideas will get you back on track.

1) Don't live under the circumstances. You are the one who controls your thoughts and feelings. Don't be a victim. Don't let others continue to wound you. Take charge of the circumstances.

   Jaycee knew her daughter Karen was sexually active, but she was afraid to talk to Karen about it. Yet Jaycee feared Karen would get pregnant or contract a sexually transmitted disease. Finally, Jaycee sat down and talked with her daughter. Karen wanted to stop having sex with her boyfriend. "That's all our relationship has become," she cried.

"I wish we could go back to the way it used to be." Jaycee cried with her daughter; then they talked about practical things Karen could do to stop and make wise decisions moving forward about her relationship with her boyfriend.

2) Learn from the past. Model how to accept responsibility for your actions. Stop blaming yourself or others. Be the best parent you can be—not perfect, just the best.

Jim is a recovering alcoholic. He has put his family through years of pain, but today he is better. Sometimes, when one of his children messes up, Jim blames himself and the years he drank. When is it going to end? Jim wonders, even though his wife keeps assuring him that many of these situations with his teenagers are normal.

3) Remember that mistakes, whether yours or your teenager's, don't represent failure. And failure is never final. See additional problems that come up as challenges and opportunities for growth rather than further attacks on you.

Carl thought he had been able to talk his son Jeff out of smoking. Carl had smoked when Jeff was little but stopped when he developed health problems. He feared for his son's health but was dismayed to see a pack of cigarettes slide out from underneath the driver's seat in his car. Knowing how hard it was to stop himself, Carl placed the cigarettes in front of Jeff at dinner and asked what he could do to help.

4) Look for influences that might undermine the healing process. Listen to what your teenager says. Is the teenager being

taunted by peers? Are health problems creating painful thoughts? Is your teenager's busy schedule becoming overwhelming?

Two weeks before school started, Kenneth woke up with a stomach ache. For the next few weeks, he was ill in one way or another. Getting Kenneth to school every day became a battle. Kenneth was tall, lanky, and quieter than most teenagers. Finally, his mother learned what Kenneth hated most about school. It was the abusive way he was treated by other students who would slam him against a locker and deliberately run into him in the hall. They had even keyed his car. Unwilling to fight, Kenneth seemed at the mercy of these bullies. Violence and being bullied in school were a reality for Kenneth.

5) Let others help. Both you and your teenager may need support from someone outside the family—this could be an adult friend, a youth minister, a counselor, or a professional—someone who can give both of you perspective.

By slamming the kitchen door, Andy announced his arrival at home and his anger over a rough day at school and at work. Later, while running an errand with his dad, Andy asked, "Could you afford for me to talk to someone like a counselor or somebody?" His dad was surprised by the question. Andy continued, "I just feel like I've lost control of my life." The first visit to a professional counselor lightened Andy's worries and his father's when they both realized Andy would get the help he needed to work through what he had been going through.

6) Delete negative talk and thoughts from your vocabulary.

"Rodney, I can't forgive my son for what he's done," protested the parent on the other end of the telephone. "You don't understand what he did."

"No, I don't know what has happened, but you are making a choice. You are saying that you choose not to forgive your son. It's not a matter of *can't*. It's a matter of will. It's a matter of something you deliberately decide to do. If you say can't, then you let negative talk rule your feelings. You are stronger than your feelings," I encouraged.

7) Focus on the future. What do you want for your teenager? What do you want for your family? Build on the strengths you see in your family. Recognize that there is always room to grow.

Jared and Judith did everything they could to save their marriage—counselors, self-help books, marriage retreats—but they finally decided they'd be better off apart. Their main concern, however, was thirteen-year-old Matthew. How could they help Matthew handle the situation? Because they were determined to keep the divorce amicable and their relationship friendly, Jared and Judith made it easier on their son.

Jared turned down a promotion that would have moved him out of town. Judith attends a singles group at church but decided not to date anyone until Matthew goes away to college. Matthew sees both parents regularly. He's already learned, however, that he can't manipulate one against the other. With a great deal of determination, this family is trying to make the best of a painful situation.

8) Love your teenager, no matter what. The late Ken Chafin put it this way: "There are few needs as strong when trouble comes as the need for the love and acceptance of parents. Because this is true it means that there is no place where there is greater potential for healing than in a family which loves and cares."[66]

●●

YOU CAN FORGIVE, FORGET, AND BE HEALED FROM YOUR PAST BECAUSE CHRIST HAS GIVEN US A SECOND CHANCE BY DYING ON A CROSS FOR OUR SINS.

●●

You can forgive, forget, and be healed from your past because Christ has given us a second chance by dying on a cross for our sins. As you seek healing, continue to ask God to help you be as gracious to others as He is gracious and forgiving to you when you make mistakes.

---

66 Kenneth Chafin, *Is There a Family in the House?* (Waco, TX: Word, Inc., 1978), 137.

CHAPTER 12

RELATIONSHIP GOALS

" I know what to do now," a gentleman stated as he shook my hand following one of our parenting events. I can't wait to tell my son that his dad has learned something that will help us both." I'm always grateful when people walk away from one of our events with at least one new tool to strengthen their family relationships. That defining moment when a new idea clicks into place gives us all hope for our families.

I hope you've found in this book some revolutionary, helpful concepts that you can apply to parenting your teenager. And I hope these new concepts have changed your way of thinking and relating to your teenager. Prior to reading this book, how would you have handled your teenager's anger? Would you have fired back with loaded words and louder arguments?

Hopefully, you realize your teenager's anger is a symptom of a neglected emotional need. You can listen to your teenager's anger and empathize with their emotion as you try to uncover the motivation behind their angry behavior. You can evaluate what need might be missing in your teenager's life. You can utilize specific actions to help meet that need. Identify one takeaway you've learned that has changed your perspective and behavior toward your teenager.

➤ A behavioral problem of my teenager involves _____
_____.

➤ The way I have dealt with the situation in the past was to ___
_____.

➤ The new way I've learned to deal with this problem with my teenager is to _____
_____.

➤ What insights have you gained in these specific areas? _____
_____

Old Way	Area	New Way
	Attitude toward my teenager	
	Discipline	
	Relating to my teenager	
	Expressing unconditional love	
	Communication	

As an interested, engaged parent, you can change the way you relate to your teenager. With time and effort, you can improve damaged relationships and restore broken ones.

••

AS AN INTERESTED, ENGAGED PARENT, YOU CAN CHANGE THE WAY YOU RELATE TO YOUR TEENAGER. WITH TIME AND EFFORT, YOU CAN IMPROVE DAMAGED RELATIONSHIPS AND RESTORE BROKEN ONES.

••

REVOLUTIONARY INSIGHTS

The old, painful, negative patterns of your relationship with your teenager were based on feelings, thoughts, and behaviors that were unhelpful and destructive. You have new insights and tools to help you respond, like the dad who exclaimed, "I know what to do now!" Here's a summary of these new, life-giving insights.

» Everyone has needs. Teenagers' needs are complicated and heightened by their developmental processes.

» Needs motivate a teenager's behavior. When needs are met in a healthy, loving way by parents or other significant adults, a teenager is more likely to respond with positive, healthy behavior. When needs go unmet by parents or other adults who could offer positive support, teenagers may look to unhealthy, destructive sources to meet their needs.

» Looking beyond the behavior to the feelings and thought motivating the behavior helps a parent discover unmet needs.

» The five gauges (Noticed, Encouragement, Empathy, Direction, and Security) provide a framework and base for determining your teenager's needs.

» Correcting the behavior of your teenager may include facing those unmet needs. It can be a learning opportunity, especially if your teenager is allowed to face the natural consequences of the behavior without your intervention.

» Meeting needs begins with unconditional love and grows from a connected, intimate relationship between you and your teenager.

» You cannot effectively meet your teenager's need unless that need has been met in your own life.

» Meeting your teenager's needs can prevent problems from occurring as well as heal problem behavior that has already taken place.

» Meeting a teenager's needs is proactive rather than passive, reactive parenting.

What other insights have you gained from reading this book?

_____

_____

_____

_____

_____

With these insights in mind, you can determine specific goals to assist you in improving and strengthening your relationship with your teenager.

In his book, *See You at the Top*, the late Zig Ziglar shares a funny but true story about goal-setting. Many years ago, Howard Hill was considered one of the greatest archers who ever lived. It was said that he could repeatedly hit a target dead center. After sending the first arrow to the center of the bull's eye [sic], he would then literally split that arrow with his next shot. As hard as it may seem, I truly believe you as a parent could outshoot Howard Hill even on his best day—even if you had never picked up a bow and arrow in your life.

You might be saying, "Zig, you're crazy!"

Let me tell you how. All you would have to do is put a blindfold over his eyes and spin him around a couple of times until he didn't know where the target was; then, I guarantee you would have a better chance at hitting the target more consistently than Howard Hill. You're probably thinking, *How in the world do you expect a guy to hit a target he can't see?* That's a good question. Now here's a better one: If Howard Hill couldn't hit a target he couldn't see, how in the world do you expect to hit a target you don't have?

Now, let me ask you a question. Do you have a target you're shooting for in your relationships with your kids? Zig Ziglar says, "It's just as difficult to reach a destination you don't have, as it is to come back from a place you've never been."[67]

---

67 Zig Ziglar, *See You At The Top* (Gretna, LA: Pelican Publishing, 1984), 147.

REVOLUTIONARY GOALS

As a parent, your overall goal is to see your teenager grow from a parent-dependent child to a self-controlled, independent adult. The specifics for accomplishing that huge task can be found in setting small, achievable goals along the way.

Why Set Goals?

» Goals provide us with direction and purpose. Without goals, we can become stagnant, repeating behavior that may leave us feeling frustrated, bored, or hopeless.

» Goals encourage us to look forward to new experiences and challenges. Setting goals forces us to stretch physically, emotionally, mentally, socially, or spiritually.

» Goals guide the way we establish priorities in our lives. For example, if the goal is to give more attention to your teenager, you may have to give up working late at night or give up some of your own personal hobbies or interests in order to have more time to spend with your teenager.

» Goals determine the way we make decisions. If your goal is to give more attention by spending more time with your teenager, then that goal helps you decide if taking a higher-paying job that requires more time away from your family is worth it.

» Goals offer security because you know where you are going and have the motivation to get there. The goal of spending more time with your teenager motivates you to get your work done at the office, so you won't have to bring it home.

» Finally, goals are a hedge against settling for the mediocre or compromising your values. With a goal, you hold out for a higher standard by living more intentionally rather than settling for the behavior from the past that may be more negative and self-centered.

How to Set a Goal

An effective goal has three parts:

1) A goal should be specific enough to be written down, clear enough to be remembered, and measurable enough to be accomplished. A parent might choose the goal of "making my teenager a better person," but how are you going to know when better is reached? A measurable goal has a specific outcome that can be examined, understood, or accomplished. A more focused goal to help your teenager become a better person might be "to help my teenager deal with her anger by giving her several coping options." Another goal might be "to support my teenager in his struggle with relationships with his friends by frequently praising his strong qualities." Set your goal high enough to challenge you and your teenager to grow. Don't set your goal so high, however, that you feel discouraged or defeated by straining toward the goal and never reaching it.

2) A goal should have a plan of steps or actions designed to reach that goal. The plan may involve only one step or several steps, depending on the complexity of the goal. For example, for the goal "to help my teenager deal with her anger by giving her several coping options," a parent might list two or three actions like these:

>> Discuss what destructive anger looks like by looking at events in the news.

» Talk about ways to cope with anger (shooting baskets, writing a letter to the person who is the source of your teenager's anger—but not sending it, talking about the situation to a good listener, confronting the person who angered you).

» Model how to handle a frustrating situation without getting angry.

The plan breaks down the goal into manageable steps, so you don't feel overwhelmed. If one step doesn't work, move on to the next step.

3) A goal should have a time for completion. Setting a time limit keeps you moving forward rather than procrastinating and getting nothing accomplished. The time limit also helps you define long-term goals that involve several months to several years and short-term goals that may be achieved in a day, a week, or a month. A long-term goal may be to help your high schooler who is falling behind academically get back on track. That's going to take time to accomplish, but there can be interim victories that move you toward your ultimate goal. You can also place a date of achievement on short-term accomplishments if you choose. Celebrate the achievement of short-term goals as well as when the larger goal is reached. If you don't achieve your goal in the designated time, don't beat yourself up. Rethink your goal and your plans to reach the goal, and set another date.

What Kinds of Goals?

Sometimes we dream about achieving a goal that is more fantasy than reality—winning the lottery, creating the world's greatest invention, writing a top-ten best-seller, starring on Broadway or in your own reality TV show—well, you get the picture. These fantasy goals are fun but not realistic for most of us. Teenagers may have fantasy goals too. As a parent, you can encourage and support your teenager's goals—whether they are fantasies or not. Many people in public positions, such as sports or media personalities, often talk about how a parent encouraged their dreams.

• •

AS A PARENT, YOU CAN ENCOURAGE AND SUPPORT YOUR TEENAGER'S GOALS— WHETHER THEY ARE FANTASIES OR NOT. MANY PEOPLE IN PUBLIC POSITIONS, SUCH AS SPORTS OR MEDIA PERSONALITIES, OFTEN TALK ABOUT HOW A PARENT ENCOURAGED THEIR DREAMS.

• •

Some goals are never discussed or defined. Sadly these goals may disappear or never get completed, not for lack of vision, but because the person never took the time to think through a goal and how to bring it to reality. The person was unwilling to make preparation, planning, and implementation part of reaching the goal. These goals may include getting a college education, owning your own home, or starting a business you're interested in.

There are many types of goals, but what I'd like you to focus on in this chapter are the goals related to your life, to your teenager's life, and to your family relationships. Take time to complete the following goal-setting activities. Give some thought to what you want to accomplish in your different relationships. You may already have started working toward a goal. Record it here. Mark your progress by using the margins to identify interim victories and short-term accomplishments. Under each category, you will find two or three examples to start you thinking.

My Personal Goals

» Goal: To restore a broken relationship with my mother by doing something for or with her
Plan: Take Mom to dinner; write a note of appreciation for what Mom did right; send flowers to Mom as a "just because" present; call her and share the events of my day
To be accomplished by (time): End of this month

» Goal: To meet a need I see in my dad's life—the need to feel cared for
Plan: Find a time to get together, just the two of us; include Dad in one of our family outings
To he accomplished by (time): By next week

» Goal: To explain to my wife why I have so much trouble showing affection to our teenagers
Plan: Share the ideas in chapters 6, 7, and 8 of this book
To be accomplished by (time): Over the weekend

» Goal: To _____
Plan: _____
To be accomplished by (time): _____

» Goal: To _____

Plan: _____

To be accomplished by (time): _____

» Goal: To _____

Plan: _____

To be accomplished by (time): _____

Goals Involving Family (spouse, other children, other significant adults, extended family)

» Goal: To strengthen or rebuild a relationship with my oldest child who lives away from home

Plan: Take eldest child to dinner and ask him to share what he wishes I had done or prioritized for our family

To be accomplished by (time): Mid-summer

» Goal: To establish a more stable financial future for my family

Plan: Ask an investment counselor to review finances; set up a budget; include family in budget planning and carrying out; establish a savings plan

To be accomplished by (time): Six months

» Goal: To _____

Plan: _____

To be accomplished by (time): _____

» Goal: To _____

Plan: _____

To be accomplished by (time): _____

» Goal: To _____

Plan: _____

To be accomplished by (time): _____

Goals Involving My Teenager

» Goal: To understand my teenager's world by getting more involved in that world

Plan: Ask teenager about sports schedule of school team; urge teenager to bring friends over

To be accomplished by (time): Two weeks

» Goal: To establish a set of guidelines for driving the car

Plan: Get teen to participate in setting guidelines; list areas of concern; write out an agreement

To be accomplished by (time): By the teenager's sixteenth birthday

» Goal: To _____

Plan: _____

To be accomplished by (time): _____

» Goal: To _____

Plan: _____

To be accomplished by (time): _____

» Goal: To _____

Plan: _____

To be accomplished by (time): _____

Part of the goal-setting process involves helping teenagers set personal goals to develop their independence. As parents, the struggle is knowing how much responsibility to give your teenager so that growth toward independence doesn't happen too early or too late. If a teenager is faced with too many tough decisions too early, she may not be prepared to handle the consequences of a poor decision. Teenagers who are given too many decisions where they continually fail may have a hard time learning to take responsibility.

On the other hand, if you maintain all the control, your teenager doesn't learn how to make decisions and accept responsibility. When teenagers leave home with no significant decision-making experience, they may make unhealthy decisions that jeopardize their future. Or teenagers who never get a chance to make their own decisions never grow up. They fail to leave home. Since goals tie into decision-making, think through these areas using the insights you've learned.

Areas where I am willing to let my teenager make decisions:

_____

_____

Areas where I am not ready to let my teenager make decisions:

_____

_____

HANGING ON TO HOPE

Mall security called Marie Citron to say that her son Maddox was being held for shoplifting. With Maddox only thirteen years old, Marie could see a destructive pattern in her son unfolding before her as she drove to the mall to reclaim her delinquent child. The store agreed not to prosecute if Maddox would work for two weekends straightening up their storage room under the supervision of his mother. Everyone agreed to the punishment.

When they got home, Marie Citron sat Maddox down and talked with him about shoplifting. Recognizing a cry for attention, she asked Maddox questions about what he had expected to happen and what he wanted to see happen. After several hours of talking, Maddox and his mother set a goal to meet Maddox's need for focused attention from his single-parent mom. Maddox and

Marie decided to spend one Saturday morning a month doing something Maddox enjoyed and one Tuesday night a month doing something Marie enjoyed. Both mother and son worked on their "togetherness" for the next six months. Marie later told me that the shoplifting incident actually brought her closer to her son than she had been in years.

Using some of the ideas I've talked about in this book, I hope you see how to teach your teenager to be an independent individual while improving the relationship between the two of you.

CHAPTER 13

CONCLUSION

A popular late-night TV host has made the listing of ten items a celebrated way of dispensing humorous information. Here's my list of the "Top Ten Things Parents Would Like to Hear from Their Teenager (but won't until the teenager develops into a mature adult!).":

10) "I don't really need a new phone, car, or latest brand-name clothing."
9) "How was your day?"
8) "I've decided not to go out tonight because I want to spend time at home with you."
7) "Thanks, Mom and Dad, for giving me rules to live by."
6) "I realize I don't know everything. I need your wisdom."
5) "I filled up the car with gas and washed the car for you."
4) "Can I take out the garbage for you?"
3) "Of course, that's a fair and reasonable punishment."

2) "I'm tired of pizza and hamburgers. Why don't we have a veggie plate for dinner?"
1) "I'd be delighted to clean up my room AND the bathroom."

Maybe you won't hear these any time soon, but I believe after you've read this book and implemented several of the ideas, you might hear something like this: "I love you, Mom." "I love you, Dad." "Thanks for being here for me." "I'm proud to be your son." "I'm glad I'm your daughter."

• •

**LIFE IS SHORT; LIVE INTENTIONALLY.
LIFE IS LONG; STAY ENCOURAGED.**

• •

As parents, you need to know that you are doing better than you think you are and that you matter more to your teenager than you think you do. Remember: Life is short; live intentionally. Life is long; stay encouraged. You got this!

Get a FREE copy of Family Shift when you subscribe to the Family Table.

Monthly mentoring
to help you raise morally
strong, resilient kids.

"A game-changer for your
marriage and your family."
-Lou Holtz, Legendary
Football Coach

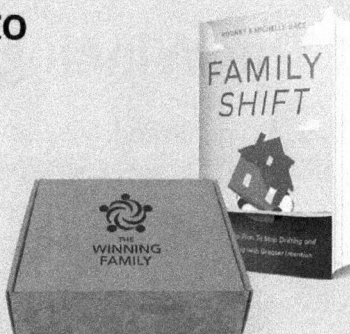

FAMILY
SHIFT

When you claim your free book, you'll also get unlimited access to Rodney & Michelle Gage's mentoring program for 30 days as a trial membership. When you subscribe to the Family Table, you will recieve:

- "Live" Monthly, 1-hour mentoring sessions and Q&A with Rodney & Michelle Gage.

- The Winning Word: A 2-minute video emailed into your inbox each week. Each video gives you a word for the week to help change the atmosphere of your most important relationships at work and home.

- Access to a private Facebook Group for community engagement, encouragement & support with other like-minded members across the country.

- Access to a private portal that features blogs, videos, courses & interviews.

- Receive The Winning Family Kit mailed to your home each quarter that contains helpful resources, recipes, and a surprise gift.

To claim your FREE copy & 30 day trail of the Family Table go to thewinningfamily.com/table

The Winning Family Podcast

The Winning Family Podcast with Rodney & Michelle Gage is designed to help you win at home. Each episode features hope, and how-to's and answers the tough questions couples and parents ask to help you win in your mostimportant relationships.

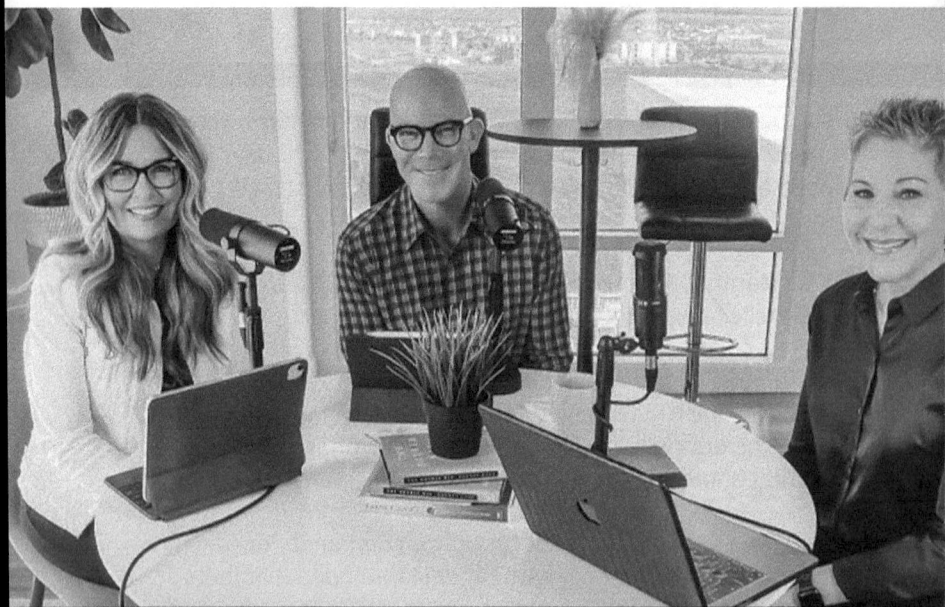

THE WINNING FAMILY
Podcast

COURSES
By Rodney & Michelle Gage

Family Shift

- 6 part video teaching features Rodney & Michelle Gage's S.H.I.F.T. Method for building strong family relationships.

- The course also includes a digital companion workbook perfect for individual and small group discussions.

The Double Win

The ideal resource to use for a small group or Lunch and Learn for your church or business.

- 9 part video teaching on the Double Win principles by Rodney Gage

- The course also includes a digital companion workbook.

- Available on Audio Pages

thewinningfamily.com

Schedule Rodney Gage to Speak At Your Church or Corporate Event.

·Schedule Rodney Gage To Speak

Throughout his 30 years as a sought-after speaker, Rodney has been featured at some of America's largest churches, conferences and corporate events. He is also the author of seven books on parent-teen relationships. In addition, he has spoken to over 2 million students in public & private schools and has been featured on over 150 radio & television talk shows.

·Family Shift Live Event

Help the families in your church, community or company "make the shift!" During this two-hour marriage & parenting event, Rodney & his wife Michelle will teach their proven 5-step framework that will strengthen and transform family relationships. This entertaining and highly engaging event will give families the insight and tools they need to start living with greater intention in their most important relationships.

Attendees will learn:

·How to agree on a desired destiny for their family and then create a plan to get there.
·Integrate family values and create a healthy culture in the home.
·How to deal with many common family issues before they become serious problems.
·How to make the shift from where they are to where they desire to be in their most important relationships.

www.ingramcontent.com/pod-product-compliance
Lightning Source LLC
Chambersburg PA
CBHW070119100426
42744CB00010B/1862